One Day Closer to God

One Step Closer to Glory

Eljaye Jobaye

FIRST EDITION

ISBN: 978-1-939748-12-6

Library of Congress Control Number: 2013949226

Published by
NewBookPublishing.com, a division of Reliance Media, Inc.
515 Cooper Commerce Drive, #140, Apopka, FL 32703

NewBookPublishing.com

Printed in the United States of America

Dedicated to Dad

You were the quintessential father and the epitome of decency. I will love and cherish your memory forever, and I will carry you in my heart and mind every day for the rest of my time on this earth. You inspire me to be a better man.

Acknowledgments

A great many people were instrumental in the completion of this book. My deepest gratitude is to my mother, father, and brother, whose love and loyalty have enveloped me all the days of my life. Thank you also to Nancy for her patience, guidance, and assistance and to Corey for the cover artwork.

Without the encouragement, cards, letters, visits, phone calls, and prayers from all of my friends and relatives who have supported me during my time of incarceration, this project would not have been possible. A special shout-out goes to Goldie, Shirley, Lois, Bev, Pat, Mert, Nora, Rollo, Marie, Barb, Sharron, and Robere.

Finally, the greatest appreciation possible goes to my Lord and Savior, Jesus Christ.

Preface

The title, *One Day Closer to God*, was chosen because its meaning is twofold:

1) Each day that we live is one day closer to death. I believe that, at the moment of death, we are in the presence of our Lord. So each day that we live is, literally, one day closer to meeting God face-to-face.

2) The title also refers to the way I feel closer to God spiritually. Each day that I spend in prison, I sense a stronger intimacy in my relationship with Jesus Christ than the day before.

Table of Contents

PHILOSOPHY OF LIFE

OBSERVATIONS

PRISON LIFE

Table of Contents, *Continued*

Introduction

The voices of the incarcerated have been either quieted or silenced for centuries. Because of this, the general populace has very little idea about what really goes on behind prison walls.

This volume will take a look at what it is like to be an inmate, from a psychological, sociological, and spiritual point of view.

I would never be so presumptuous as to think that I am a spokesman for all prisoners in our country today. I simply want to share my perspective on doing time. I have done over twenty-five years now and still have the rest of my life to do yet.

I am in for a crime that I did not commit, and I am but one of many innocents in our nation's prisons and jails. Justice may not be served on this earth, but in the world to come, there will be perfect justice.

Through the power of the Holy Spirit, I have dedicated my life to Jesus Christ. I let His Will guide me all the days of my life. He has a purpose for me, like He has a purpose for each of you. Everything I do, I do to bring glory to God. May you be blessed as you read the pages of this book.

PHILOSOPHY OF LIFE

Chapter 1:

Love and Charity to Others

In the summer of 1967, the Beatles sent a message to all the world when they premiered their new single, "All You Need is Love." The communication was written in many different languages at the coming-out party, and it was purposely broadcasted to every nation. The statement that the Pied Pipers from Liverpool were trying to make was that, if people would release the hate in their hearts, drop their weapons, and show love to their brothers and sisters with whom they share this globe, then this would become a much better and more livable planet.

The Fab Four's proclamation was laconic, yet powerful. If you think about it, they hit the nail right on the head: All we really do need is love. Can you imagine what a paradise we would live in, if every man, woman, and child would rid their minds, bodies, and souls of hate, bitterness, estrangement, malice, scorn, revulsion, loathing, abhorrence, detestation, aversion, and antipathy? Of course, that will happen after Jesus comes back to create a new heaven and a new earth.

You have all heard that "love makes the world go 'round." But what does "love" *really* mean? Everybody seems to have a different definition of it, not to mention a different perspective on it. To be sure, there are many different kinds of love, and you will feel the emotion in a unique way, based upon your own past experiences.

Most people would agree that some common characteristics of love would include caring, kindness, unselfishness, charity, tenderness, and affection. As human beings, we have a deep, innate need to be loved and to give love. If we are deprived of either, the results can be devastating.

People who have a dearth of love in their lives grow to be emotionally stunted, and are consumed with negative emotions such as anger, bitterness, jealousy and hatred. They want to lash out at society and at anyone who appears satisfied and happy. They feel that they have been cheated somehow, and that life "owes them something."

Well, nobody ever said that life was fair, and it certainly isn't. I don't know of one person who has never experienced struggles, setbacks, defeats, problems, and unhappiness. These things are simply part of the fabric of life. God gives us these challenges to make us strong and to build the kind of character that He desires.

Many metals have to go through a tempering process before they are usable. So it must also be for God's children. Our Lord never promised us a bed of roses. In fact, Jesus said we must "take up the cross daily" and follow Him. That is a pretty tall order; we can only imagine how arduous a task it must have been to carry a cross. Of course, the statement is a metaphor, but it is a command for us to fight the good fight here on earth against Satan, his demons, our own flesh, and every imaginable temptation of sin.

We cannot do this by ourselves. Only with the help of our Heavenly Father, the Holy Spirit, and our Lord and Savior Jesus Christ can we overcome all of our enemies. We can do nothing constructive without the Triune God, but there is nothing we *can't* do when we have Him in our lives.

The Bible mentions love throughout, and one of the most famous verses comes at the end of the "love chapter" of 1st Corinthians 13. In verse 13, Paul states, "And now these three remain: faith, hope and love. But the greatest of these is love." This clearly shows the great importance that the Lord places on love.

Human love is not the same as divine love. We cannot fathom the depth of love that our Heavenly Father felt that caused Him to send His only Son to earth to die for the sins of mankind. Jesus, the Creator of the universe, Who sits to the right of the Father on His Holy Throne, humbled

Himself and became flesh. What a tremendous sacrifice that was! To lower Himself by living a life as man, knowing the betrayal, torture, and agonizing death that lay before Him, and still willingly doing it so that mankind could have salvation is the ultimate in love. What greater love is there than to lay down your life for your fellow man?

We can learn a lot from Jesus' example. He is our Role Model, whom we should strive to emulate as closely as possible. Of course, all of us have sinned, and we live in a world dominated by evil. But if you look at our Savior's life closely, you will see that everything He did, He did out of love. He healed the sick, gave sight to the blind, forgave the repentant, cleansed the demon-possessed, and raised the dead. The statement that "God is love" is factual, for all love flows from the holiness, righteousness, and goodness of God. Without Him, love itself would be impossible.

How can you apply these concepts in our modern world today? Treat all people with the love, respect, and consideration that they deserve.

Show mercy and forgiveness to someone who has wronged you, just as God has done. Strike up a friendly conversation with a complete stranger. Spend a day with a youth who needs an adult mentor. Volunteer at a senior citizens center, a day care, a nursing home, a food shelf, a scout troop, a soup kitchen, a Salvation Army outlet or Red Cross office, a Little League team, or thousands of other worthy charities. Call or write a friend you haven't seen or talked to in a while. Repair any broken friendships or relationships you might have.

In short, show as many kindnesses as you can, as often as you can. Also, do it for purely altruistic reasons and not because you expect anything in return. If you dedicate your life to this concept, there will be a renaissance of good will, the likes of which has never been seen. Love is contagious. Who knows? It might spread like wildfire to all the corners of the globe!

I know there are a bunch of you cynics out there saying, "That all sounds real nice, but it is completely unrealistic." This may be true, but if everyone brightened his/her little corner of the world, think how much better life would be. Not only that, but our Lord would be very pleased to see that His children had overcome wickedness and were living their lives according to His precepts.

Chapter 2:

The World is Evil

All you have to do is look around, and you will clearly see that the world we live in is dominated by evil. Every possible sin imaginable is prevalent on our planet today: deceit, lust, envy, violence, greed, gluttony, sloth, indifference, selfishness, hate, defiance of God, arrogance, conceitedness, and many more. There seems to be no end to the wickedness. Every newspaper, TV or radio newscast, or any other news medium seems to always carry a plethora of stories in which the Prince of Darkness has had his hand. Evilness makes news; goodness doesn't. Malevolence piques interest; benevolence doesn't.

If you don't believe we live in a nefarious place, just examine the evidence. Headlines blare of heinous crimes, misanthropy between nations and ethnic groups is at an all-time high, the downtrodden have become pariahs in our "success-at-any-cost" lifestyle, people disparage each other in every possible social situation for no discernible reason. Even friends and relatives are contentious with each other.

What other craven mischief can be found in the hedonistic world society? We have become a dissolute people, full of debauchery and lewdness. Pornography is ubiquitous: It is available in books, magazines, films, sex stores, peep shows, cable TV, telephones, strip clubs, and the Internet. That is just what is available today. As the telecommunications industry continues to evolve, the availability of stimuli that caters to the basest desires will become even greater.

There are conflicts in many parts of the globe as despotic rulers look to neighboring countries for more land and power. Sometimes the struggles are within homes, as members of the same family fight against their flesh and blood in a battle of wills.

Divorces and separations continue to be commonplace. The devil attacks the basic family structure because he knows that that is where the morals, values, and religious truths are taught to children in their formative years. If families crumble, then can society, in general, be far behind?

In short, we have acted in an ignominious manner.

Why are humans so sinful and decadent? The answer lies in the Garden of Eden. In the creation of the cosmos, everything that God made was perfect. He even made man in His own image. At first, Adam and Eve lived in perfect harmony with each other and their surroundings. It was only after they ate of the forbidden fruit of the Tree of Life–at the serpent's urging–that they fell in disfavor with their Creator and were banished from paradise.

Mankind is naturally evil and born into sin because of the Original sin in the Garden of Eden.

Our nature and tendencies are diametrically opposed to the Holy Deity. When we transgress, we give in to our Self, and indulge our desires. It is an easy thing to do; in fact, it seems like the easiest thing to do in every circumstance. Jesus says in Matthew 7:13; "For wide is the gate and broad is the road that leads to destruction, and many enter through it." The road to hell is always going to be the easiest route to take. That is why there are so many treading its path. It is fun to be sinful and to be "of the world." Why did Yahweh give us the ability to sin?

The Holy One, in His infinite wisdom, decided to give humanity freedom of choice. He did this because He desired for us to *want* to worship, praise, and love Him, rather than having a bunch of robots bowing down to Him by edict. It makes sense that He would want His prized creations to adore Him of their own free will. But, with choice, comes the possibility of choosing darkness instead of light, impiety instead of righteousness, the Evil One instead of our Lord.

In order for there to be a choice, the Great

Architect had to allow Lucifer and 1/3 of the angels to sin and thus, fall from heaven. Our Heavenly Father gave Satan (his name changed after his fall) dominion over the earth. That doesn't mean, however, that The Fiend has *carte blanche* to do whatever he wants. The King of Kings always has ultimate control over what happens anywhere in the celestial sphere. Nothing happens without His knowledge and approval.

Given that, why does The Ruler of the Universe allow suffering and all of the negative things in life? For millennia, this is a question with which the human race has struggled. There are many possible answers. It might have something to do with the fact that we tend to reach out more to Jehovah when tragedy strikes in our lives.

When everything is going great, we feel like we can handle life on our own, and Our Maker gets squeezed out. Our priorities become: How much wealth can we accumulate? What next material thing should we purchase? Where should we go on our next vacation? What great investment opportunity is available right now, so that we can keep worshipping the almighty dollar?

We are playing into The Tempter's hands by putting ourselves first and forgetting about our Author, Protector, and Savior. How quickly we forget about The Lord of Lords when life is going along swimmingly. But, when the walls start falling down around us, to whom do we cry out? Even atheists and Satanists wail for assistance from The Almighty when push comes to shove. Why? Because, deep down, we all know there is a Supreme Being greater than us, and we will all reach out to Him in a real crisis as a last resort.

Our God is full of love, mercy, grace, and forgiveness. He doesn't want anyone to spend eternity in hell, in exile from Him. Hell was explicitly built for The Father of Lies and his demons. However, because the Man Upstairs is holy and just, He can't allow sin in His presence. In order to remedy that predicament, He sent His only Son, Jesus Christ, to die on the cross for all the sins that human beings have committed throughout history. Someone had to pay the enormous price for all of those offenses by atoning for them. Jesus, because He was without fault, was the only qualified surrogate sacrifice His Father could accept. Through our Redeemer's death and resurrection, we are reconciled with our Master.

We have an inherent need to have a Godhead in our lives in order to feel complete. Our souls–our real selves–belong to Him, and yearn to return to Him in some way. Our souls will live on after our physical deaths, because that essence of our individual selves is immortal. Where that soul resides for eternity is determined by each of us individually.

In order to go to heaven, I believe that we must believe in the Lord Jesus Christ, make Him our personal Savior, and repent of our evildoing. Without the blood of the Lamb of God to wash away our iniquities, we would stand in filthy rags on Judgment Day and be sentenced to damnation. We cannot "earn" our salvation through good works, prayers, or any other human endeavor. Only through grace, God's gift of undeserved love, are we saved. All we have to do is accept that gift and make Him the number-one priority in our lives.

As a species, we have become contumacious to The Judge. We have rejected His Law and have decided that we don't need Him. After all, we can do such remarkable things in this Space Age/ Computer Age/Technological Age. We are masters of our own destiny, right? Don't we have all the answers with all of our great medical advances and treatments? Haven't we explored the oceans' depths, the tops of the highest mountains, the craters of the moon, and the other planets in our solar system?

Don't we have supercomputers which run nearly every aspect of our lives with incredible accuracy and efficiency? Don't we have bombs and missiles that can destroy our world many times over? We are so advanced, so powerful, and so intelligent; what do we need God for? Aren't we self-sufficient, the way things are now?

We are in dire trouble if we think that we don't need the Triune God. Compared to the majesty and power of The Divine, we are microscopic.

He created the cosmos and everything in it. He is omnipotent, omniscient, and omnipresent. There is nothing that He can't do. He knows everything that will happen in the future.

We are His creation, and we owe Him our lives, our souls, our bodies, and our faith, adoration, and praise. We should worship Him and pray to Him unceasingly. We should renounce the Prince of the Air and his fallen angels, and turn away from the immorality in our lives. We need to put ourselves in God's hands and live righteous lives. Only then can we achieve total victory and receive the Crown of Life.

Chapter 3:

Looking for Something

Everyone is looking for something in life. We need certain things in order to feel complete. In Chapter 1, it was mentioned that each of us needs to love and be loved. Without love, we become empty shells with no vibrancy. We might be able to exist, but the quality of life just isn't there.

So, other than love, what is everybody searching for? Many would answer "happiness." But, how do you obtain that fleeting feeling of euphoria? There are many roads that lead to it, and you must each choose your own way to get there. You have your own definition of gladness. You may find it in money, power, fame, or adulation. Others may find it in their family, career, sports, or TV. Whatever makes you happy tells a lot about what kind of person you are.

Unfortunately, you may pursue felicity by participating in activities which are destructive to you. Prime examples of these would be the abuse of drugs, alcohol, gambling, food, the Internet, and sex. Folks can become addicted to almost anything. There are so many different pleasurable possibilities available that the options are infinite.

Why is it in our nature to be on a quest in the first place? One reason is because life itself is filled with great deal of pain. Ineluctably, we all have to face our impending mortality. In addition, we also have to deal with the loss of family members, relatives, close friends, acquaintances, classmates, and family pets to the ultimate thief–death. The Grim Reaper robs us all of these relationships, and we have to somehow come to grips with the fact that death is a part of life. Knowing that, though, doesn't make the void created in our lives any easier to fill.

What else causes anguish, which makes us long for something to assuage it? Physically, there seems to be no end to the diseases, syndromes, cancers, viruses, bacteria, fungi, parasites, and other maladies that attack the human body. Even though modern medicine has come a long way in the last century, there is still a multitude of pathogens that we cannot cure and/or treat. We even seem to have new ailments constantly appearing out of nowhere! We may be stricken by these conditions, or perhaps it will be one of our loved ones whom we have to watch suffer.

One of the deepest emotional pains is the loss of romantic love. Nearly everyone experiences this agony at least once in a lifetime. Perhaps you are in love with another person, and that love is unrequited. Or maybe a couple will build a loving relationship, get engaged and married, but over time, it becomes stale and loses its fire and splendor. The break-up between a couple who are supposedly committed to each other for life can be very traumatic to all parties involved. Some never overcome the devastation, and their lives fall irrevocably apart.

If we are not concentrating on avoiding torment, then we have a proclivity to contemplate on things that make us feel complete. In fact, one way to look at life is to think of it as a journey. The destination varies from person to person, but we are all on this thrill-ride together. We have to look out for one another and help each other as much as we can along the way.

Some people find fulfillment in their families. They dedicate their time, energy, and resources into becoming the best father, mother, husband, or wife that they can possibly be. That is a very noble pursuit, and one that is all too uncommon in our world today.

Each member of a family needs to feel loved, valued, heeded, and appreciated. Often, the oldest members are ignored, and their opinions fall on deaf ears. Why is this? Our society strongly favors the youth subculture, and most of the mass media and advertisements are geared toward teens and young adults. Appearing youthful translates into beauty, and "thinking young" equates to being "hip."

Some cultures value you more the older you are, but ours is just the opposite. Once you reach a certain age, your value plummets, and you become "disposable." We often house our elderly in nursing homes and other venues suited strictly for the Golden Generation. The decision to do this is often out of love, but it keeps them out of sight and segregates them from mainstream America.

This alienation is a tragedy because senior citizens have a lot to offer the rest of us. Not only can they regale us with stories, anecdotes, and happenings from a bygone era, but they also are a source of tremendous knowledge and wisdom. We sometimes forget that we have new experiences and learn new concepts every day. Just imagine what an impact an accumulation of several decades worth of these valuable nuggets could have on the young people of today! And let us not forget the incalculable sacrifices they made in overcoming The Great Depression, World War II, and the Korean conflict.

This is a forgotten and neglected segment

of our population, and these wrongs should be rectified immediately. I am a fifty-something individual, and I think the time-honored should be given a special, elevated place in our society. They should be listened to, included in social activities, and assisted in every way possible (medical, travel, ambulatory, companionship, financial, etc.).

On the other side of the spectrum, the youth continue to be vilified for many evils, when only a small percentage is actually participating in them. They are watched more closely in stores because the clerks are worried about shoplifting. They are given exorbitant car insurance rates simply because of their age. They are lumped together because of stereotyping, instead of being viewed on an individual basis. Sure, there are some bad apples, but they should pay the price, not the innocent people in their demographic.

Young people are our future, and they deserve to be treated with respect and love. They should have their opinions heard, and they should have input on the burning issues of the day. The worst travesty that can be done to any segment of a commonwealth is to take away its voice in matters; nothing makes a person feel more helpless and ineffectual.

Other groups who are discriminated against are those with physical and mental limitations. These include those challenged from birth, or due to infections or injuries. Also in this group are the obese, who suffer a myriad of unfair abuses, which result in a high cost to their self-esteem. Why do we treat people who have characteristics different from ourselves in such a shameful manner? Maybe it is because they remind us of our own imperfections and shortcomings.

Maybe it is because it raises our own sense of self-importance when we "knock down" those less fortunate than ourselves. We look down our noses on the impoverished, homeless, and less-educated. We like to think it is their fault that they can't pull themselves up from their bootstraps and become self-sufficient, instead of being a burden on the tax-paying stratum of society.

We need to show more compassion to every person. We should aid them in any way possible, whether the need is physical, psychological, emotional, or spiritual. Every living soul has value; therefore, we should not "give up" on anybody. Sometimes you may just need a "hand up" and, after that, you can take care of yourself. The able-bodied should not just have a hand out for a handout, but they should pull their own weight for the good of the whole. It's only fair.

The earth is full of temporal objects. They, along with our physical bodies, will wither away someday and be reduced to dust and ashes. However, there is one thing that we can search for that is a true and eternal axiom: Only God can give true redemption and real satisfaction. Everything else will pass away, but our Father in heaven is Someone Whom we can always count on to be there for us. He will never forsake us or stop loving us. He is a Father Who wants all of His children to come to Him, even the ones who have gone astray. He is the Good Shepherd Who wants to collect all of His flock and bring them safely home.

What are *you* looking for in life? Have you found it yet? Is your life complete, or do you feel like there is something missing? You can try all of the man-made paths to bliss, but when you finish with them and still do not feel sated, then try the Divine Way. That is the Way of Truth, the Way of Hope, and the Way of Salvation. Only then can we find what we are ultimately searching for: The Alpha and Omega, Who always was and always will be. Our Creator, Jesus.

Chapter 4:

Everything is Relative

Albert Einstein gave us the Theory of Relativity, and he was absolutely right: Everything really is relative, if you think about it. Each human being has a unique point-of-view of the world. Depending on the circumstances and a person's life experiences, a single event can have a myriad of different perspectives, all personalized to each individual.

Time is a paradigm of this. A perfect day spent with a loved one will seem to fly by, while a brief moment of excruciating pain can seem like an eternity.

I have always been a person who likes clear, sunny, warm days. Most people would probably consider that "ideal weather." As you may have noticed, clouds are not a part of that equation. Clouds represent stored moisture. Even if they are fair-weather cumulus clouds, they still can blot out the sun and interrupt your sunbathing. Besides, sunny weather seems to lift everyone's spirits and moods; it makes you feel good to be alive.

But a funny thing happened one hot, sultry summer day. Both the air temperature and the relative humidity were flirting with the century mark. It was a day unfit for any living creature; I only ventured outside because I had no choice. I stared up into the light blue sky, looking for any kind of respite. Then I saw them: a congregation of giant, white cotton balls were drifting aimlessly. As they floated across the sun, a huge shadow glided over the land. The heat was abated by several degrees, and all organisms seemed to breathe a collective sigh of relief. It was the break for which nature was hoping. I never thought I would be thankful for a cloud, but I sure was at that moment!

I realized, for the first time, that clouds actually had some value. More importantly, I learned a very valuable notion: Most things, ideas, and concepts can be positive or negative, contingent on the moment in question.

A similar illustration can be made in regards to wind. It plays havoc with most outdoor sports like tennis, golf, baseball, football, and fishing. A strong draft can literally ruin picnics, and we all know about the destruction tornadoes and hurricanes can cause.

So, when is moving air beneficial to have around? Let's go back to that 100-degree day. A nice breeze sure would have done wonders in providing some comfort. A zephyr would also help keep the mosquitoes away. Maybe you want to fly a kite or sail a boat. You need a strong current of air to do those activities. Wind can be very useful given the right circumstance.

Trees have been cut down in the name of progress for centuries. If a farmer wants to plant his crops or let his animals graze, the forest needs to be leveled. For a city to be built, many woodlands need to be sacrificed to make room for houses, streets and highways, and businesses. Branches and trunks can become homes for unwanted pests or, during a storm, flying projectiles.

There are many worthwhile uses for timberland. Flora represents some of nature's greatest resources. They provide an eclectic list of shade, protection, beauty, wood, and oxygen. Where would we be without them? They enhance the aesthetics of a yard or mountainside. They protect farmsteads and houses from storms by acting as a windbreak. Who hasn't sat under a large tree in the shade and drank a cold beverage on a summer day? We also receive products like lumber, paper, pulp, cardboard, plywood, etc.

One of the main reasons environmentalists want to preserve the Amazon Rainforest, other than the preservation of the vast diversity of wildlife, is the enormous amount of oxygen it exudes. Everyone knows that humans have a symbiotic relationship with plants because we trade carbon dioxide for their oxygen. We couldn't survive without each other.

These three examples evince that it is only in the eyes of the beholder and the situation itself that determine whether a particular item is beneficial or detrimental. Since perception is so important, we are in control of our outlook on life. We might as well view it with a sense of purpose in striving for the highest moral good.

Chapter 5:

THINGS ARE GRAY

Life would sure be a lot easier if everything were black and white, but that is not the case. Very rarely can you accurately use the absolutes "never" or "always" in any given situation. Things in this world are capricious and generally fall into the gray area.

Indeed, the only true constant in the universe is God's love. It is unchanging and unconditional, just as our Creator is the same yesterday, today, and tomorrow. We can depend on Him at any given time to always be there for us.

Even when we encounter situations that appear clear-cut, most often are not. They are abstruse.

There are two sides to every coin and to every story. The salient thing to do is to try to look at things from other people's points-of-view. If you can figuratively walk a mile in their shoes, then you will be in a better position to empathize with them. You can then better comprehend their standpoints and ameliorate any disagreements, instead of only trying to refute the opposing positions. What a wonderful society it would be if everyone would sit down, take a minute, and try to understand others better and be more cognizant of their feelings.

One example where there is a difference of opinion is this scenario: A guy takes his girlfriend to a dance. When he goes to buy them drinks at the bar, he sees that she is off dancing with some other dude. Her beau gets angry and confronts her when the dance is over.

Who is right? They both are. He went out on a date with a girl for whom he has deep feelings. Of course, he would feel hurt by her lack of loyalty to him.

On the other hand, they weren't "going

steady" or dating mutually exclusively. Another man asked her to dance while she was just sitting there all alone. She innocently wanted to go out and have some fun. You can clearly see how an innocuous encounter can have far-reaching ramifications if not dealt with appropriately through open communication.

Things are gray in relationships.

Another illustration is politics. Citizens should be actively involved in politics in order to have a voice in the affairs of government and to effect positive change. In this country, the Republicans and Democrats have dominated the political scene for many years, creating, in essence, a two-party system.

Some radical, dyed-in-the-wool extremists of each coterie find it impossible to find anything good about the other faction. They castigate, excoriate, and calumniate each other. Neither side has a monopoly on policies that are perfect for the American people. There is plenty of disingenuousness on both sides. There are certainly some "good" and "bad" planks in both party platforms. Just like there are many respectable and contemptible candidates representing each bloc.

Whichever group is presently in power, the other alliance will criticize what the current administration or Congress is doing, even if they have no better ideas of their own. If the nation is going through a crisis, the camp that is in control will try to convince the American people that there is a silver lining in the dark clouds. The minority party will say the sky is falling.

Both cadres will promise anything to get elected, then often backpedal and make excuses once they are in office. They become so entrenched and drunk with power that they scoff at any proposed term limits.

Issues are gray in politics.

Religion is another hotbed for controversy. Many people are ardent followers of their particular faith and adhere to their tenets with a fever-pitched zeal. While being intense in your fervor to your spiritual beliefs can be a good thing, it is also pertinent to keep an open mind in regards to different denominations and other religions. Take the time to study them exhaustively and speak to adherents to gain a first-hand explanation. You just might be surprised of how much you will learn, and your eyes will be opened to new ideas and perspectives. Maybe you have a lot more in common with the other person than you thought, and your differences will seem more trivial.

Does that mean you should question God and any of His commandments? Absolutely not, because He is infallible and perfect, and so is His Will. This is where fervid faith comes into play.

It's easy in our humanness to wail to the Lord, "Why?" I've done it myself many times when catastrophe struck. We must be audacious and trust in Him, despite whatever ordeal is in our path. There is a reason for whatever circumstances in which we find ourselves.

The important thing to remember is that our Maker has a plan for each of us. Someday, when we get to heaven, we will be able to discern why everything happened to us the way it did.

Religion is also a gray area.

These three instances are just the tip of the iceberg of all that is not 100% one way or the other. Look around you and see for yourself. Instead of being resolute and obstinate, let's conjoin and try to be tolerant and broad-minded in dealing with our fellow inhabitants. Maybe they will also come to realize all the many shades of gray there really are.

Chapter 6:

Smell the Roses

There is an old saying that says, "Stop and smell the roses." We have all heard that phrase, but what does it really mean?

Our society today is extremely frenetic, which can be noisome. It seems like nobody wants to have to wait for anything. We drive swiftly to our jobs, we eat quickly in order to get to our next appointment, we text/talk hastily on our phones, we need high-speed computers to assist us in our jobs and home life, and we channel-surf with our remote controls because we can't endure watching commercials.

We are constantly in instant-gratification mode; we cannot abide any idle downtime. As the pace continues to move faster and faster, it seems like the stress in our lives increases commensurately. Look at all the maladies that have exploded in recent times because of the increased pressure we put on ourselves.

In short, we are impatient to a fault, and we want our desires without having to wait for them. If we have to wait for any interval of time, we get peevish and agitated.

Along with the additional aggravation that is self-imposed, there is opportunity cost by not slowing down and experiencing all that life has to offer. Yes, technology has enabled us to live in a hyper-world with the invention of cell phones, computers, and other techno-toys. But do we really need to treat these things with apotheosis? I would aver that we miss a great deal of existence if we go through it too rapidly to enjoy the minutiae.

Have you ever stopped to stare at the clouds and try to figure out what the formations resemble? Have you sat on a porch, patio, or deck and listened to the birds sing? Have you watched a sunrise or sunset during a pensive moment? If you live near a large body of water, have you watched and listened to the waves roll in on the beach? Have you gazed at some majestic, snow-capped mountains?

Whatever your method of getting away from the complexities, conundrums, enigmas, and turmoil of this planet, ease up and take the time to enjoy many of life's simple pleasures. How can we do this?

There are many options available, including several types of meditation. The general idea is to clear your mind and concentrate on just *being*. By focusing on nothingness, and relaxing your body through deep, rhythmic breathing, you can alleviate much tension.

Exercise is another path to stop and smell the roses. I love jogging, and as I go around the track, I plan, in general terms, the direction where I want my life to go. I also notice nature in all of its gorgeous splendor. In autumn, the distant trees' hues are spectacular. Sometimes, there are also numerous kinds of animals flying, calling, or scampering nearby.

The best time for me to stop and ponder is late at night before I go to bed. It is the only time of the day when it is peaceful and serene. I go over what transpired earlier that day and think about what is in store for tomorrow. I don't plan any further in the future than that because it's too painful to bear.

Naturally, the best way to spend some "alone time" is with God. That means reading the Bible and letting the Holy Spirit give you revelation as to what the Word is saying. It is a living book, and each time you read it, you will notice something new. You need to be assiduous in seeking Him. The Lord will speak to you and give you direction for fighting the good fight.

Another way of spending time with Jesus is through prayer. Think of it as a conversation between you and the Almighty. One venue I pray in every day is the shower stall. I find it the perfect place to speak with my Heavenly Father.

Some suggestions for prayer would be to praise Him for being holy, merciful, and full of grace. We ought to thank Him for forgiving all of our sins and for His abundant blessings. We should bring petitions to Him that are weighing on our hearts because He will ease our burdens. He wants to have a personal relationship with all of us, and we should strive to get to know Him better.

It is easy to get caught up in the frantic, frenzied hubbub of our modern world, but it is in our best interest to take some personal time for ourselves and become insouciant. Some people like to be nostalgic and reminisce on fond memories. Perhaps you might think of a dear friend, family member, or significant other. Whatever that moment of reflection may entail, you owe it to yourself to enjoy life to its fullest by stopping and smelling the roses.

Chapter 7:

Simple Things

What is important in life? It's the simple things. Unfortunately, the common misconception is that you need material wealth, high social status, power, and fame to be considered a "success." Those are the goals and ambitions that Satan wants you to strive for because they are all about promoting your "self." He wants you to devote all of your time and energy in the pursuit of being a megalomaniac, so that you won't have any time for what is really paramount in the grand scheme of things.

It is a clever con into which many people feed. It works because we, as humans, are selfish by nature and want to feel important and superior to others. But we must try to eschew worldly things and remember that they are only temporal.

You may have heard the saying, "The best things in life are free." In many ways, that's true. Think of all the activities you can do that don't involve spending a lot of money. There are an infinite number of ideas that fit into this category.

First and foremost, there is worshipping God. This can be done by attending church, participating in a Bible Study, or having family devotions. Sometimes it may be something as easy as a heartfelt prayer. The key thing is to give the praise to where it belongs: our Triune God.

For what are we without our Savior? Only through Him is there eternal salvation and hope for the human race. The marvelous thing is we can give glory and be laudatory to our Maker at any time and any place. In order to build a personal relationship with Jesus Christ, we need to talk to Him regularly and often, and invite Him into our hearts.

Then there is being with loved ones. No

matter what your version of "family" is, spending quality moments with them is very rewarding. Certainly your spouse or significant other deserves a great deal of love, time, attention, and affection. You have made a lifetime commitment to your marriage partner, and now you are one flesh in God's eyes. Treat that person like you would yourself, and do everything for him/her from a place of unconditional love.

There are many simple romantic things you can do together. One of my favorites has always been taking a long walk outside, hand-in-hand, on a gorgeous day. This gives a couple a chance to talk in a comfortable, relaxed setting, and it also allows them to observe our Creator's handiwork up close. They might eye beautiful trees or flowers in their full glory, see some breathtaking vistas, or chance upon some animals in their natural habitat. It doesn't cost a cent to enjoy nature's beauty.

If you have children, utopia might be taking them on a picnic or camping trip. Kids love to play games outside and run around. These excursions give them a chance to have a hearty meal, breathe in some fresh air, burn off some energy in a healthy way, and bond with other members of the family.

Have you ever sat around a roaring campfire telling stores and singing songs? How about roasting hot dogs, marshmallows, or S'mores? There is nothing like being sprawled out on a blanket enjoying a picnic basket full of delicious food, listening to the sounds of the Great Outdoors. These relaxing outings will help you abrogate all your everyday tensions.

Maybe you just want to "hang out" with your friends. You might want to play a sport together, such as baseball, basketball, football, soccer, or hockey. If the weather is inclement, the options might include playing cards or a board game indoors. Sometimes just sitting around having a good conversation or listening to some tunes is an ideal way to spend a few hours. Of course, there are always video and computer games to play, not to mention watching TV or DVD's. To touch base, you might phone, text, instant message, or e-mail someone you care about.

If you happen to be alone, you can use your solitude by ruminating about how to achieve equanimity. You might get philosophical and think about profound things. You could dream of ways to improve the world around you and aspire to do noble things, such as random acts of kindness and "paying it forward."

The bottom line is this: Don't get caught in Satan's trap by being too self-absorbed. Signs of this are acting proud, arrogant, conceited, narcissistic, or greedy. Diffidence is the key. Be humble before God and man and live an unpretentious life, full of guileless pursuits. You will find that they are truly the most satisfying and fulfilling.

Chapter 8:

More is not Better

One of the most prevalent themes in today's climate is that more of the good things in life is always better. We are constantly being bombarded with the message that our lives will be more pleasurable and gratifying because of them. This is the devil appealing to our basest desire of avarice (one of the seven deadly sins). Down deep, we all want more of the finer things that life has to offer. Sometimes, our drive to obtain them becomes insatiable.

Money is supposed to be the "answer" to all of our problems. The more that you have–by any means necessary–the happier you will be, we are told. This is the Big Lie perpetrated by the Prince of Liars. He wants us to put ourselves before God.

Sometimes, the affluent live godly lives and are munificent to the church and to charitable causes. Others, by living with material surfeit, show self-centeredness and contempt for those who are living in want and abject poverty. Some millionaires throw a few dollars to charity to make them feel like they've "done their duty." Why don't they volunteer at a soup kitchen or a Salvation Army and really get to know the homeless and destitute on a personal basis?

There is nothing inherently wrong with being "comfortable" or even rich. We all strive to accumulate enough wherewithal to have financial security, a nice house, a car, and enough money for the needs of our families. Working hard in order to obtain the "American Dream" is a noble and worthy ideal. Having a lot of money or material goods is not evil or sinful in and of itself. It's only when the drive for and the love of riches get in the way of putting the King of Kings first that the line into iniquity has been crossed. Remember the Lord said in the First Commandant that He is a jealous Deity, and we should not put anything before Him in our list of priorities.

There have been countless extremely well-to-do persons who have led very miserable existences. Look at how many lottery winners have been hit by one tragedy after another. Some have blown their winnings in a short time and are soon bankrupt. Easy come; easy go.

They also get hounded relentlessly by family, friends, and gold diggers who come out of the woodwork for a piece of the largesse. Also, they have to worry about what to buy first and how to hold onto their newfound wealth. They get consumed with obtaining luxuries and forget about what's truly important. Sometimes they even end up taking their own lives because they are in such despair.

As you can see, having financial success is no guarantee of living a charmed life. Without real substance like faith in the Holy One, the love of family and friends, and showing beneficence to the less-fortunate, you can become jaded and empty. After the partying and the fake companions fall away, what will be left? Just loneliness, after putting all your eggs in one basket of temporary, ephemeral, and transient pleasures.

The Bible says in Matthew 16:26, "What good will it be for a man if he gains the whole world, yet forfeits his soul?" Matt. 6:19-21 adds, "Do not store up for yourselves treasures on earth...but store up for yourselves treasures in heaven...For where your treasure is, there your heart will be also." Garner Jesus' favor instead of living for the moment.

Doesn't it seem like there is an overabundance of advertising on T.V., radio, print, billboards, and all other mass media? We also seem to be saturated with college football bowl games. When seventy programs go, it dilutes the thrill and honor of being invited.

Maybe your excess of choice is gluttony. Considered another of the seven deadly sins, this is eating or drinking much more than you need. There are millions starving in the world every day who would give anything for a morsel of food. Even in developed countries like the U.S., there are many suffering from malnutrition and hunger. The moneyed nations throw away tons of nutritional food on a daily basis. It's one of the great tragedies of our time.

Then there are overindulgences to addictions like drugs, alcohol, smoking, and sex. Drugs may provide a short-term high, but you will have to come down sooner or later. And when reality hits, life will seem even bleaker than before. Not only that, but the toll on the body by illicit drugs (or even by abusing some prescription ones) over time can be devastating. You could wind up with severe brain damage, in a coma, or possibly dead.

Intemperance of alcohol, too, can wreak havoc on the body through prolonged use or by bingeing. Many of your major organs are affected, not to mention the increased risk of being in an accident. Abusers of drugs and alcohol are much more likely to commit serious crimes because of their lack of inhibitions.

Smoking tobacco has been a health hazard for many decades, not only for the users, but also for those in their vicinity through second-hand smoke. It, too, affects the major organs, especially the lungs. Exercising regularly, eating a balanced diet, and quitting smoking are three of the best things you can do to help keep your body healthy and fit.

Being concupiscent with sex is another unhealthy behavior. The rise of AIDS and other sexually-transmitted diseases has made casual sex a life-and-death decision. Other consequences include being charged with “date rape,” having an unwanted pregnancy (which could lead to an abortion or years of child support payments), or jeopardizing a potential relationship. Sometimes one or both of the parties involved are not emotionally ready for it or are too young to understand all of the ramifications.

All of these examples show that moderation is the key to healthy living. Let’s not become rapacious in our appetites. We should just be content and satisfied with what we have instead of wanting more. We should be abstemious to the abundance in our lives.

When we look at the impoverished around

us, we should realize how blessed we are with all of the resources at our disposal. We should be thankful to the Almighty for amply supplying all of our daily needs and giving us bounteous lives. All things belong to the Great Architect, and we are merely caretakers of His possessions. If we just put our complete faith and trust in Him, we will truly be the richest ones on the face of the earth.

Chapter 9:

Nostalgia

Nostalgia is both valuable and underrated. Many people warn that you shouldn't "live in the past." But they forget that our background is what makes us the human beings we are today. Oftentimes, our childhood determines what kind of adults we become. Life experiences shape our current outlook on everything around us. Even ordeals and difficulties can make us stronger in the long run. Mistakes can help us learn important lessons in order to avoid them in the future.

Reflecting about cheery occasions is good for the psyche. It warms the heart with recollections of dear ones who have passed on. We can find great comfort in the fact that our Christian loved ones are communing with Jesus right now. As long as we hold onto these close friends and relatives in our thoughts, they will continue to live in us.

Sometimes a certain scent, song, or image will act as a mnemonic, and will spark recognition of a specific person, place, or moment. It gives you a warm feeling and puts a smile on your face when you recollect a cheerful memory. It's God's way for us to experience a wonderful piece of our history over and over again. Souvenirs, mementos, tokens, trophies, and other keepsakes mean so much to the owner because of the sentimental value attached.

I'll freely admit that I am a very nostalgic person. I enjoy reminiscing on a copious amount of fond memories, full of memorable instances and precious people.

Some of my favorite nostalgia include:

1. Going on family vacations to many parts of the country
2. Bowling and playing baseball, softball, basketball, football, soccer, volleyball,

tennis, floor hockey, and golf

3. Collecting stamps, coins, and baseball cards
4. Playing a plethora of card and board games
5. Fishing in the summer and hunting in the fall
6. Having fun with friends and relatives
7. Learning to play the piano at age five
8. Attaining the rank of Eagle Scout
9. Traveling to Europe for five weeks when I was 15-years-old
10. Playing trumpet in the high school marching band and at church for special events
11. Participating in declamation in high school
12. Attending numerous music concerts
13. Learning to appreciate the music and influence of the Beatles
14. Cheering for and promoting the USC Trojans, the Los Angeles Lakers, and the Boston Red Sox

15. Receiving a B.A. degree in accounting from a leading, private college
16. Realizing my dream by living in San Diego and savoring the Southern California lifestyle
17. Working as a Payroll Supervisor at a major corporation at the age of 24

At times, I have been accused of being too smaltzy, maudlin, or mawkish. That's Okay; I am comfortable being a sensitive guy who cares deeply.

There is nothing wrong with longing for the "good old days," as long as you don't lose touch with present-day reality. If you completely transport your consciousness to an earlier era, then you could be suffering from a severe mental illness.

In the same vein, you should not rest on your laurels and keep reliving old glories. If that's all that matters to you, you are depriving yourself of a dynamic, exciting existence in the here-and-now, not to mention it could squelch any future dreams and aspirations you might have.

Let's keep things in their proper perspective: The past is awesome on which to reflect, the present is what we should concentrate on the most, and the future should hold all of our wishes, ambitions, and goals. Remembering this will help us make sure we don't stress any one part too heavily. Life is about balance, and our viewpoint concerning time is a significant part of that.

Of course, being in prison creates an aberration as to the prospect of time. Because the current circumstances are so harsh and painful, remembrances of the "outside" is almost all that the incarcerated have in which to cling. As a defense mechanism, the mind blocks out the draconian hell behind bars and becomes numb to the constant, unrelenting suffering.

Many men have no freedom in their future because they are never getting released. Given that environment, it's very easy to give up, climb into a shell, and shut out your surroundings entirely.

My future is in my Savior's hands; therefore, I have heaven and salvation assured to me. In that hope, I live trying to make this world a better place for others. I've taught GED and college classes for over sixteen years to help hundreds of inmates improve their education and develop life skills. I have mentored mentally-challenged convicts so that they can function on a daily basis and meet any challenge head-on.

I try to show love, compassion, consideration, kindness, and generosity each day to those with whom I interact. I feel that's how the Lord would want me to do my time. I have tried to use my duration being locked-up in a positive, constructive manner and help my fellow man at every juncture. With the Holy Spirit's guidance, I plan to continue on that same path for the rest of my days in here.

OBSERVATIONS

Chapter 10:

JOY VS. HAPPINESS

Every person has an innate desire to be gladsome and content. We all search for utopia, but very few even approach it. We will do almost anything to secure it, yet it remains elusive. Why is that? The answer lies in the fact that life is challenging, difficult, and arduous by its nature. It is that way because, as a species, we have rebelled against the Creator and brought these hardships on ourselves.

We are an afflicted ilk because we have fallen far short of God's ideal. He is a just Deity, thus He demands perfection. We're all in need of redemption. As punishment for our frailties, we must contend with the consequences of Original

Sin by living in an imperfect, unfair, and flawed world. In Genesis 3:17-19, Jehovah said to Adam after he ate the forbidden fruit, "Cursed is the ground because of you; through painful toil you will eat of it all the days of your life. It will produce thorns and thistles...By the sweat of your brow you will eat your food."

As was discussed in Chapter 3, felicity is a temporary state of euphoria that can be caused by a myriad of things. Maybe your marriage is working out great and your spouse is everything you ever wanted in a mate. Maybe your children have many wonderful accomplishments that make you proud of them.

Maybe you have reached stratospheric heights in your career, and you have high social status and prestige. Maybe your school or favorite sports team won a championship. Maybe you have many loyal friends and family members who really care about you. Maybe you have plenty of financial resources, material goods, and get to travel all over the world.

Whatever brings you a modicum of bliss,

cherish that. Hold onto it and appreciate how it enriches your reality. The problem, though, is that cheerfulness is fleeting, desultory, and earthly. It can only bring you momentary pleasure, not true lasting fulfillment.

Even those who seem to have it made, have their share of problems. The divorce and suicide rates among celebrities are astronomical, and these are individuals who have an incredible amount of fame, fortune, and power. Yet they are some of the most desolate and depressed people on earth. How can this be? The answer is simple: They need Jesus Christ in their lives.

If you have the Lord in your life, then you will experience something that is infinitely more rewarding than mere mirth: pure, unadulterated joy. The difference between the two is that happiness comes about because of your circumstances and is man-made, while joyfulness is strictly heaven-sent by the Triune Godhead. We cannot manufacture it ourselves; it is a supernatural gift from an ever-loving Supreme Being.

How can elation be described? It's impossible to put into words: You have to taste it in order to fully fathom it. To have a personal relationship with the Messiah means becoming a new creation. He said in John 3:3, "I tell you the truth, no one can see the Kingdom of God unless he is born again."

He gives us this remarkable, unearned gift of blessedness free of charge just by asking Him into your heart. Non-Christians can never understand having tears stream down your face and having a lump in your throat because you are so emotionally overcome by the touch of the Holy Spirit. The impetus for this might be singing praises to the Almighty, getting an important prayer answered, listening to another believer's testimony, having a loved one escape injury or recover from sickness, having the Divine One lead you in a meaningful endeavor, or fellowshipping with other adherents.

The bonds between brothers- and sisters-in-Christ are eternal, and there is no feeling like it. If you are looking for beatitude, and not just merriment, there is only one way to obtain it: Make the King of Kings the ruler of your existence and place your faith and trust in Him. He will give you more delectation than you can possibly imagine.

Chapter 11:

Real Friends

Real friends are some of the most valuable loved ones you will ever have. There is an inherent need to form interpersonal connections with others. The reasons for this can be varied: the desire for companionship, the want of intellectual stimulation, or the gratification that a letter, card, poem, phone call, e-mail, text, or face-to-face encounter brings.

There are many types of friendship. You may have just met an acquaintance, yet feel enough of a bond has formed to consider that person a pal. Sometimes, it takes no time at all to feel an attraction to, or a high degree of comfort with, another individual.

Why is that? Everyone has a unique, diverse body chemistry, and people either naturally "mix well," repel each other, or they are somewhere in-between. You have all experienced it: For some inexplicable reason, you like or dislike others the instant you meet or see them.

This might help explain why a human being has an inborn tendency or inclination to gravitate toward certain companions. Sometimes, you just don't "mesh" with another. No matter how hard you try, there is only a particular level of familiarity that you are destined to reach.

I've been blessed with tremendously wonderful friends throughout my lifetime: childhood, high school, college, San Diego, business associates, and even in prison. Each one is very dear to me, and I have enjoyed a meaningful relationship with all of them.

There is a special place in my innermost being for every buddy I've ever known, and I thank God for each of them. None of them will ever know how much our interaction has positively affected my time on this earth. I treasure the fun memories we've created, and I wish they could know how much I love and value each of them as a person.

It seems like when everything is going sensationally, and there are no bumps in the road and is clear sailing ahead, everyone wants to be your *amigo*. But, when disaster strikes and catastrophe occurs in your life, which of your so-called chums will stand by your side through thick-or-thin? Who are the pretend "fair-weather" buds, and who are your *real* friends?

I am loathe to admit that some who were close to me in the outside world are no longer associated with me. I realize we all have choices to make, and it's easy to discard a comrade if you don't feel you receive enough in return. They didn't want to invest time, energy, effort, expense, and space in their minds, when all I could offer them was my undying gratitude. When they weighed what they gave versus what they received, they realized the scale was tilted against them.

It's our sinful, evil nature to only want to do what's best for ourselves. So, what happened was that I quietly vanished from their collective consciousness. Out of sight; out of mind, I guess. No grandiose pronouncements, no explanations, no apologies were given as to why they chose to slip away.

That is the cold, hard reality of prison life, but I'm still devastated and surprised by those who have fallen away. I always thought they would be on my side, no matter what. If the roles were reversed, I would immediately offer them my full support. You really find out who your backers are when you are in crisis mode.

Then there are the ones who not only stand 100% behind you, but increase their support when they know you especially need it. It all comes down to one word: loyalty. What a powerfully uplifting quality to possess! One who is loyal to another exhibits character, integrity, honesty, courage, and honor. It takes scruples, intrepidness, and moral fiber to back a person, regardless of the accusations leveled against him.

The fact is, they know the suspect a whole lot better than anyone in the corrupt justice system. If he claims to be innocent, they believe him without waiting for exculpatory evidence. They don't need to ask questions or learn all the details in order to have faith that he isn't capable of doing what was alleged.

Developing companionships in the "joint" can be a bit tricky. So many guys like to play con games and mind games, that it can be hard to judge their true motives. Most will try to lure you in, in order to obtain something from you.

However, there are surprisingly a fair number of quality men living in our penal system today. These confidants can be some of the closest mates you will ever have because of the "foxhole effect." This is named after the intense nexus that is formed between two men sharing a foxhole during the heat of combat. With bullets flying overhead and bombs exploding all around you, you feel a certain intimacy with whomever is sharing the same stressful circumstances.

That's the same profound bond that is forged between convicts sharing their painful daily burdens. Whether I get released or not, many of the men I've befriended in here will be thought of as lifelong brothers because of our common trials and tribulations.

I have tried to be a good friend to all, but any relationship is a two-way street. In order to receive the benefits, you need to do your part and give generously, graciously, and cheerfully to meet the emotional needs of your companion. You will feel satisfied by doing it, and your fellowship will be strengthened by the love you exhibit. To have a friend, you first have to be a friend. Sometimes, that might mean accepting and putting up with their annoying habits, foibles, idiosyncrasies, and shortcomings. Remember, we all have them because we are all imperfect. Real friends are truly worth their weight in gold.

Chapter 12:

Gratitude

Gratitude is a mind-set that exemplifies much consideration and humbleness. It means being touched by the thoughtfulness of others. The kindness shown can be anything from a minute gesture all the way to an incredible sacrifice. No matter the size of the gift, just the fact that somebody cared enough to spend the time, energy, and expense on your behalf ought to be enough for you to acknowledge the favor and show appreciation for it. This can be done at the time of receiving it or at a later date.

My parents instilled in me at a young age that it was perfunctory for me to write a thank-you card for every gift I received. Being thankful for all things was considered paramount. It was a valuable lesson which I learned for a lifetime, and it is a trait that is still very significant to me, and one I've always tried to show.

None of us is so important that we should take other people's kind acts for granted. You might receive an inkling you are about to receive something, or it could be a total surprise. Who doesn't like to be surprised with a beneficence?

One of my biggest pet peeves is those who show ingratitude. It should be an automatic response to be thankful for a solid done on your behalf. Just a simple "thank you" or "much obliged" lets your benefactor know what is in your heart. It's a win-win scenario: The recipient feels inspired, and the giver feels uplifted. It doesn't take much effort, but it makes a world of difference.

Why is it meaningful to show appreciation? For one thing, it is simply the polite course to take. There is a paucity of good manners in today's world, and it is rarer still in prisons and jails. Any courtesy done in the penitentiary is highly unusual and seldom expected or seen. I always try to say "please," "thank you," "excuse me," "your welcome," and all of the other niceties, given the right situation. Some inmates chastise me for this, but I tell them that just because we are locked up doesn't give us license to do away with manners of civilized society.

It seems that morals have decayed greatly across the board over the last forty years. Today, people are ruder, more inconsiderate, and more self-centered than in previous generations. As the world becomes more and more malevolent, we should be vigilant for Christ's return. Jesus said in Matthew 24:37, "As it was in the days of Noah, so it will be at the coming of the Son of Man."

Another reason to show thankfulness is that it is a way to express how you are feeling. You want to let others know you are grateful for what they have done for you. If you don't confirm the favor, you may not receive anything from them in the future.

If you send a present to your loved ones, and they don't acknowledge it, two problems arise. First, you don't know if they received it in the first place. Second, you don't know if they appreciated the thought or the gift itself. Either case can leave a bad taste in the giver's mouth. The odds are that it will be the last offering the negligent party will receive from that person. If I go out of my way to do an indulgence for a friend or relative, I expect them to at least show a modicum of recognition. It doesn't take much to let me know how they feel.

Of course, we have an entire holiday devoted to gratitude: Thanksgiving. I like the tradition of going around the dinner table and having all attendees say for what they are thankful. We should be cognizant that Our Provider grants everything (including life itself) to His children, according to His Will.

Benefaction should always be shown to our Maker. Paul says in 1 Thessalonians 5:16-18, "Be joyful always, pray continually; give thanks in all circumstances, for this is God's will for you in Christ Jesus." Our entire lives should be lived in a state of perpetual thanksgiving toward

Him. What does He want from us? A humbleness that demonstrates who we are in relation to the Almighty. It pleases Him when our hearts are brimming with gratitude for our abundant blessings. That's why I'm heartily grateful.

Chapter 13:

Masculine vs. Macho

When you are incarcerated, you instantly morph into "survival mode." This entails doing whatever it takes to exist in an extremely harsh, rigid, and dangerous environment. This is a form of macho posturing.

That may mean "puffing" yourself up to appear bigger, stronger, meaner and crazier than you really are. Many animals in nature do the exact same thing; examples include the cobra with his hood and the puff adder performing his namesake maneuver.

Psychologically, it makes a potential adversary think twice before engaging you in combat. He normally won't attack unless he thinks he can beat you handily, with minimal risk of getting hurt himself.

Machismo denotes exaggeration in acting male-like. It is taking all the male qualities to the "nth" degree, such as the bully mentality.

Some females are attracted to this aberrant behavior, despite the fact that a machismo guy tends to treat the woman in his life in a very dominating manner. Because of the heightened sense of his own importance, he feels that he is far superior to members of the fairer sex, and his actions reflect that.

He is more likely to be verbally and physically abusive. When he comes home from work, he expects his lady to wait on him hand-and-foot. It never enters his mind to help with "feminine" duties like cooking, cleaning, washing, or taking care of the kids, because he thinks those chores are beneath him.

He treats his significant other like an object, such as forcing her to dress in a way that pleases only him. The woman must always know her place and never express her opinions or thoughts if they are contrary to her man's. His view on life is sophomoric and immature.

In the twisted machismo world, when it comes to lovemaking, the experience is strictly all about giving him pleasure. There is no giving on his part, only selfishly taking. She is to be obedient to all of his commands and attend to all of his needs, without any regard to her own. For her, having perfunctory sex is an empty, hollow pastime. For him, it is just another symptom of the disease known as misogyny.

He also treats his children with the same indifference and disdain he shows his wife. Every activity has to be approved by him, and his point-of-view is always "right." He is obdurate, stubborn, inflexible, dogmatic, and he rules his home with an iron fist and daunts anyone who gets in his way.

Being masculine, however, is completely different. It encompasses all of the positive male characteristics, but only in moderation. It is being a "man's man:" someone other men admire, respect, and emulate. Not only do they enjoy his presence, but most women consider him the quintessential mate. Why?

Because he is suave, debonair, cosmopolitan, and sophisticated. He is not rough around the edges, but smooth and sensitive. He does not come across as effeminate or weak, but is manly by showing caring, consideration, gentleness, and kindness to all living things.

He puts his spouse's needs before his own because of his unselfish spirit. He is a giver, not a taker. His mission in life is to make his mate happy, satisfied, and fulfilled, even to his own detriment.

He may be ostracized by his male peers for acting masculine instead of macho because they are jealous. Despite that, he doesn't change what he stands for, and doesn't let others dictate to him how he should think or act.

The masculine dude also puts his progeny before himself. He works hard and toils each day to bring home a healthy paycheck in order for his offspring to have a better life. He is heavily involved in his kids' lives by participating in sports with them, getting to know their friends, talking with them during meals and in their rooms, and taking an interest in how their education is faring. He gets to know all of his children's hopes, dreams, aspirations, and goals. They feel safe under his watch because they know that he would lay down his life in an instant for any one of them.

He is well-liked and respected everywhere he goes because he doesn't have an inflated ego and is not self-absorbed. He is secure in his manhood and has no enemies because he shows respect to all. He is assertive, not passive or aggressive. He has a love for nature and all its creatures. Everyone gravitates to him because he is fun to be around and says interesting, intelligent, and humorous things. He doesn't tear down other people by using insults, criticism, coarse jokes, or profanity. He is open and honest about his belief in God and enjoys speaking on religious matters.

If you are a guy, which kind of man exemplifies you? If you're not happy with whom you see in the mirror, do you have the courage, perseverance, and fortitude to change? If you are a woman, which kind of man appeals to you? If you are a minor child, what kind of man would you want as a father?

The world doesn't need any more macho men; we have too many already. Let's hope and pray that the males on this planet will demonstrate more masculine traits and fewer macho ones.

Chapter 14:

Water–Necessary and Harmful

Water is one of the most important substances on the planet. Without it, life itself would be impossible. That's why astronomers were so excited about finding ice on Mars; it meant that there was a possibility of life there.

But conversely, hydro can also be terribly destructive. If you have ever experienced a major flood, monsoon, hurricane, or severe thunderstorm, you know firsthand how devastating it can be. Don't underestimate its raw power or take fresh, clean water for granted. It might not always be as readily plentiful as it is now.

In order to survive, water is essential for all plants and animals. It is one of life's building blocks and performs a variety of functions for the betterment of each individual organism. Every cell in your body needs an adequate supply of H_2O on a regular basis, so it is not surprising that it makes up a high percentage of your body weight.

If you do not get enough, your brain will send the message of overwhelming thirst. If you go long enough without replenishing your fluids, your organs will begin to shut down. The weather conditions, such as the intense heat of a desert, can exacerbate the dire situation. Dying of dehydration must be one of the most agonizing deaths imaginable.

It is also very important to make sure your pets have plenty to drink so they don't overheat. When you're leaving for any length of time, make sure their water dishes are full.

Water is needed if you want to grow your own plants. Both urban and rural inhabitants enjoy a healthy lawn of green grass, as well as hardy flowers, fruits, vegetables, trees, and bushes. A farmer certainly knows the value of a well-timed downpour when his crops are wilting in the field. He also knows it's critical to give his livestock plenty of liquids, especially on hot days.

A drought is a worry for just about everyone (unless you live in a rainforest). It brings with it the added danger of grass and brush fires because of the tinder-dry conditions.

Many large cities of the world are found on major bodies of water because their ports were primary centers for trade and transportation. Because of the burgeoning growth of the earth's population (the latest estimate is over seven billion), the demand for clean, potable water continues to skyrocket. States out West are fighting over a limited supply, and they have even started rationing it in some locations.

In some Third World countries, a dearth of fresh, uncontaminated water is the cause of millions of deaths. In addition, waterborne illnesses such as cholera and dysentery become epidemic in squalid locales that have little or no water sanitation and rampant insalubrity. Also, there are the horror stories of scary-looking parasites that can invade your body through tainted aqua.

Scientists say that there is roughly the same amount of water in the world today as there has always been. The explanation is found in the water cycle that keeps the same water rotating through its various stages. For example, it might start out as a nimbus cloud that drops its precipitation during a thunderstorm. It fills up oceans, seas, lakes, rivers, and ponds. It always runs to the lower ground elevation until it fills up a larger body of water.

If the precip falls on land and soaks into the soil, it is then filtered down to the aquifers found at the water table several feet below ground. It can then be brought up to the surface through the use of a well.

The bodies of water continually lose their moisture through the process of evaporation when it returns to the sky to form clouds. Then the whole process is repeated ad infinitum. In a cold climate, snow or sleet would fall instead of rain or hail, but the idea is the same.

With the advent of the "green" movement, conserving water has become trendy and a metamorphosis has taken place. It is now fashionable to buy a rain barrel and catch your own fresh water. After several calamitous decades of heavily polluting our waterways, we now stop and treat our wastewater before dumping it. We need to take even better care of our natural resources before we reach the point of no return.

Many use water for recreational purposes. You might fish in a lake or stream, or go waterskiing or boating. Others may just go sunbathing on the beach, while listening to the waves crash on the shore.

Three-fourths of the planet is covered with water, but all except for a small percentage is salty ocean-water. This leaves only freshwater lakes, brooks, and underground reservoirs to get drinkable water. There have even been wars fought over *agua*.

Moisture can be very destructive to wood,

books, or other paper products because it warps, wrinkles, and discolors. Too much in a home can attract molds and mildews, which can be costly to have removed. It also attracts unwanted insects, mice, and other pests, so it's a good idea to prevent having excess sources around in order to keep away the creepy crawlies.

We should always respect any amount of water and treat it with the seriousness it deserves. Every year there are many drownings. Some are caused by accident, suicides, or just plain carelessness.

Water is mentioned throughout the Bible. Jesus said in John 7:37-38, "If anyone is thirsty, let him come to Me and drink. Whoever believes in Me, as the Scripture has said, streams of living water will flow from within him." John the Baptist declared in Matt. 3:11, "I baptize you with water... He will baptize you with the Holy Spirit and with fire."

PRISON LIFE

Chapter 15:

Current Situation

We are approximately half-way through our journey together. In the previous fourteen chapters, I have shared with you some of my philosophies of life and observations pertaining to a wide range of topics. I hope this gives you a better idea of where I'm coming from.

Now I would like to switch gears and focus on what life is *really* like behind bars. As I stated in the introduction, very few people in the free world have any idea what goes on behind the walls, fences, barbed wire, razor wire, and locked doors of our nation's brigs. It is a domain you have to experience first-hand to fully understand.

I wouldn't wish this hell-on-earth on my worst enemy. But the public needs to be told the truth, and the only ones who can tell it are incarcerated 24/7.

I had to make a decision whether to explain in detail the true, unvarnished, objective account of prison life. The alternative would have been to sugarcoat the experiences and living conditions I have seen to make it more palatable to the masses. I decided on the former because I think you, the reader, deserves the frankness, candor, and honesty that only verity can bring.

None of what you are about to read is made-up or hyperbole, but is unbiased fact, to the best of my knowledge. Now, be forewarned, that in order to give you an accurate description of the extremely negative atmosphere an inmate must deal with daily, I am going to come off sounding like a growler and a grumbler. I'm neither. However, I'm willing to take that gamble in the interest of being thorough.

Also, for simplicity's sake, I'm going to intentionally generalize what happens in here.

In chapters 18-22, I will go more in-depth and share some personal anecdotes. Obviously every institution is unique and does things differently. Stereotyping is unfair, and we should form opinions on an individual basis because each person is nonpareil.

But, for our purposes, I will talk in more expansive terms. I will not use any specific names in order to protect everyone's anonymity. I'm also going to sprinkle in some hoosegow lingo, slang terms, and monikers of actual prisoners I've met during my sojourn in order to give you a flavor of the environment.

In the first three chapters of this section, I will give you an overview and introduce the basics. After that, I will get into specifics by demarcating five disparate viewpoints: mental, physical, emotional, social, and spiritual.

The last section of the book, comprised of four chapters, deals with the Almighty and our relationship with Him. I will touch on God's Will, a quilt illustration, little things that matter in the spiritual realm, and finally, our blessed forgiveness found in the Person of Jesus Christ. May the remaining chapters open up your collective eyes, hearts, and minds to Him.

When I first got arrested, I was completely naïve about the justice and penal systems. Because I had never been in trouble before, I didn't even know the difference between a prison and a jail. I had no clue what a Grand Jury did; or what an arraignment, indictment, or Voir Dire meant; or what omnibus, Frye, and Rasmussen hearings were. I learned so much the hard way.

Obviously, most criminals have no respect for authority, law enforcement, or the laws of polite society. Their selfish, anti-Establishment thinking is what brings most of them here. The pen is a bastion for hate-mongers, bigots, reprobates, bullies, sadists, and the dregs of the body politic. Unfortunately, some of the bullies' victims end up here as well because they are severely traumatized from their abuse. You see evidence of this every day.

Even though I've lived a law-abiding life and do not have a "criminal mind," I have a great affinity for convicts. I share a deep bond and have a great deal of empathy for them after living in the trenches together for over twenty-five years.

Hollywood movies and the media paint a certain portrait of life in the slammer. My favorite ones are *The Shawshank Redemption, The Green Mile, Lock Up,* and *An Innocent Man*. But don't get the idea that the depictions are faithful just because that's what you're told to believe.

If you get convicted of a crime, you are sentenced to a period of time in a jail (one year or less) or a prison (more than a year). You are locked up in order to keep the populace safer and to exact punishment for the alleged crime.

Being in stir doesn't only mean losing your freedom. You can also lose your humanity and identity. You forfeit every right you cherish and hold dear when you enter the walls. You probably took them for granted, because, throughout your lifetime, you've always had them, and now they are maliciously torn from you. What if you never get released or be reunited with friends and family again, or taste the sweet nectar of liberty, freedom, and personal choice?

It is the state DOC (unless you had a federal conviction) that makes houses of correction such nightmares to the hapless individuals who end up there. They dehumanize you by assigning you numbers, a castigation that the Nazis perfected. The more the guards, staff, and administration can think of you as subhuman, the more pain they can inflict in good conscience. They sometimes go out of their way to cause anguish and suffering in an inhumane manner. They even have harsh penalties against staff who get too friendly with offenders.

What this does is foment anger inside your mind during your incarceration. By the time you are released back to the streets, you aren't rehabilitated (the "powers-that be" gave up on that long ago). Instead, because of your built-up rage, it's possible that you could go out and commit an even more heinous crime.

Of course, events like these don't always happen. I'm not advocating phasing out clinks because there is a certain segment of the population who really *needs* to be locked up, possibly for a lifetime.

I'm just saying, treat prisoners more humanely, and increase the educational opportunities (GED and college), job skills, treatment and vocational training. That kind of positive programming would definitely increase the odds of an inmate becoming a productive, tax-paying member of the community someday, instead of re-offending. If no one gives you a chance or a glimmer of hope, you could go back to the wrong crowd/gangbanging and become a recidivism statistic.

The "Big House." Doing "hard time." Whatever you call it, living in such an adverse milieu for a long period of time can do irreparable harm to your psyche, body, personality, spiritual beliefs, self-esteem, and hopes for the future. It is both grueling and exhausting, not to mention mentally taxing. It is definitely a marathon, not a sprint. If you are foolish enough to go too hard and fast, you will find yourself prematurely burned-out and spent.

It is an extremely intense, petty, depressing, loud, oppressive locale with numerous irrational, illogical, onerous, fatuous, harebrained, moronic rules with which you have to deal. That is a big reason why you develop a "we vs. them" attitude with your captors.

The pokey is a very lonely place. The lack of human contact and a dearth of friendly faces really comes with an emotional price. One of the hardest things about doing time is being separated from the ones you love. That separation is the perfect breeding ground for families crumbling, relationships breaking, and friendships straining. The system is set up to isolate you by taking away your support system of outside contacts.

You never really get used to the "cooler," and it never gets any easier. It is very unnatural to lock up a human being in a cage. I'm still uncomfortable in these surroundings after all the time I've done. If anything, with my advancing age, I'm less able to tolerate the stress, noise, juvenile antics, and DOC policy-makers.

My current situation is being a resident of a

medium security adult correctional facility. I have done time in two county jails and four prisons so far, all on the same bit. The possible custody levels are maximum (having a long sentence or committing a major infraction behind the wall), close (more than ten years yet to do or a treatment failure), medium (less than ten years left), and minimum (less than eighteen months left). The security becomes less stringent as you progress to lower custodies.

This place is not for the faint-of-heart, and even the stoutest, most intrepid souls have weak moments because of the extreme nature of the venue. Everyone is scared when you first come to the "jug." It is the fear of the unknown, in addition to dealing with a heavy concentration of some of the most violent people on the planet. That can be a bit unnerving.

To my amazement, I've met quite a few decent guys in here. In fact, some of my best friends I met in the joint. That was anomalous to me.

Felons quickly develop reputations and

roughly fall into two categories: those who are constantly conning and scheming, and those who just want to do their time and be left alone. Guards are also divided into two camps: those who feel it is their duty to pillory and make life more difficult for their underlings, and those who do their job and treat their charges humanely.

You learn from the get-go to watch your back and be aware of who is behind you at all times, to be wary of guys who act a little too smoothly, and to read body language, gestures, and facial expressions to pick up important clues. It helps to not be a loner (there is no anonymity, and there are negative ramifications for being reclusive) and to have comrades who will back you up in case of an emergency, just as you would help them. There are many predators in this jungle who are always on the look-out for easy prey, just like in the animal kingdom.

There is inmate-on-inmate violence all the time. You are miserable, bitter, saturnine, angry, and feel hopeless and helpless. You lash out in order to salve your profound, enduring wound found in the core of your being. The easiest target, and the one with the most lenient consequences, is to attack someone weaker. You may not even know him. Even the sports are fierce and ultra-competitive.

Someone once told me that chickens will peck to death any of their kind that become sickly or injured. The same mentality is prevalent in the "slammer:" If you get labeled as a victim for any reason, the vultures will pile on and make your life unbearable.

It's kind of like a small, self-contained town: Everybody knows your business, and gossiping about juicy tidbits is a common pastime. By being inquisitive, you can find out personal info and use it for extortion (if you are in on a bad case, that becomes your "jacket").

Many thugs are professional mendicants who live off the kindness of others. They don't want to spend their own money, but would instead rather harass by being a parasite.

Evilness is everywhere. Tough guys are strong-arming and intimidating the timid;

the slick are playing con and mind games; the perverted are raping, sexually abusing, and telling ribald jokes; the profane are cursing profusely and using the Lord's name in vain; and the furious are assaulting, stabbing (using homemade shivs and shanks), and bludgeoning. This is the harsh reality in the can.

You can't afford to have a bad day in the keep, much less a bad moment. Many of the men you interact with are walking time bombs, a hair-trigger away from exploding in a torrent of unspeakable ferocity. You can't lose your temper and lash out verbally or act out physically, without receiving swift retribution. A wrong glance, an inadvertent bump, or a word taken out of context are all examples of innocuous mistakes that can lead to harsh, brutal consequences. Dudes will even sucker-punch you instead of fighting "fair." There is no honor when it comes to vehemence.

There are no comforts or luxuries in the "coop." Everything is hard, difficult, and arduous, including the rules, inmates, guards, staff, and administration.

Loud, raucous noise and rampant profanity are ubiquitous. It is so exceedingly vulgar that I probably hear the "m-f" word an average of 10,000 times a day. It is a word I despise, and I cringe when I hear it. It really takes a toll on your outlook after a while.

You have no privacy whatsoever. You have to use the toilet right in front of your cellie (the guy with whom you share your cell), and anyone else who just happens to be walking by your window. It's against the rules to hang up a curtain or cover up the window because of security concerns. You are expected to use a "courtesy flush," which means flushing continuously to avoid unwanted odors.

You have to undergo "full-body" strip-searches every time you enter the county jail, go on a writ, have a visit, go to segregation (a.k.a. "the hole"), have a lock-down, or take a random urinalysis test (which could be anytime day or night). The phones are monitored, your mail is read going in and out, every conceivable space is bugged, and you are scrutinized when you're in the visiting room.

The vast majority of outlaws have a "street name" they use as a nickname. Some of the more colorful ones of wrongdoers I've met are Gizmo, Roach, Lefty, Greaseball, Fluffy, Sweets, Deuce, Zeus, Doughboy, Cat Scratch, Shorty, Slim, Joker, Jackpot, Kid Rock, Blade, Ghost, Country, Creep, Dummy, Bam, Capone, Youngin', Silk, Kilo, Broke-back, Half-dead, Fast Eddie, C-note, Heavy, Bigs, Beefy, Monkey, Chucky Monkey, Wood Tick, Profit, Greedy, Pluto, Circus, Little Daddy, Homocide, Burnie, Tree, Flames, Song, Shadow, Fresh, Kirby, Hound Dog, Ice, Mafia, Top Dog, Big Dog, Meechy, Afro, D-Nice, G-Ball, Mess, Dirt, Holy Pimp, Break Bread, Junebug, Tweaker, Gutter, Killa, Q-Burger, Turtle, Hoss, Snako, Stoney, Tone, Spike, Nacho, Trigger, Mellow, Shopping Bags, Chill, Meaty, Bear, T-Nutty, Niño, Trey Guns, Criss Cross, Clutch, Mosquito, Pit Bull, and my favorite, Can't Get Right.

Here are a few common slang colloquialisms (many of these you'll also hear in the youth, hip-hop culture). "My bad" is "I'm sorry." "Good lookin' out" is "thank you. "4-1-1" is the same as information. "5-Oh" is code for police. "Pulling your chain" is analogous to messing with someone. "That's what I'm talking about" means something good just happened. "I like that in you" is a compliment to another. "Bogard" is another word for strong-arm.

"Run that" or "bet that" is equal to "go with it." "Let me holler at you" is said instead of "let's talk." "True dat" is equivalent to "that's right." "Straight up" is the same as "I'm telling the truth." "Handle that" or "go on a mission" means to attack someone. "What's good?" is used in lieu of "What's happening?" "Hook a brother up" means "give me some food." "Homey don't play that" is used in place of "I don't do something like that." "Put me in the car" is "let's throw-in together on a meal."

"Three men and a stranger" is when your partner in cards is secretly sabotaging you because he is in cahoots with the other two players. "You're trippin'!" is "You're losing it." Out on front street" means putting another guy's business out in public. "Wham whams and zus zus" are sugary snack items in the commissary. "Sugar in the tank" is the same as being effeminate.

Spending a lot of money is "living large." "Put it on your skin" is similar to "Make an oath." "He is good people" is used for "being a stand-up guy." To "get salty" or to "spin out" is equal to losing your temper. If food is "fire" or "Al," that means that it tastes awesome. "Flip the script" is akin to changing something 180 degrees. "Grill" is teeth.

"Stuck like Chuck" is another way of saying that you're in a bad situation. "It's all good in the hood" is the same as "Everything's all right." A cigarette is called a "square" or an "L7." To "spark" means to smoke. "Starvin' like Marvin" is saying you're really hungry. To "smash" food is equal to eating hungrily. "Keep it on the down-low" is code for "Don't tell anyone."

"I got you" is the same as "I'm going to pay you back." "Kick rocks" is akin to "Get out of here." "Jump Street" means the beginning. "Feed the warden" connotes to defecate. "Mello" is a friend. "Off the chain" is another way of saying "outstanding." "Fresh catch" equals a new case. "Flipper" is a loser. "Getting some work done" is code for tattooing. "Get in where you fit in" is akin to "Get comfortable."

"Something, something" means a little bit. "Ticket to kick it" is a green light to talk. "Out of pocket" connotes that you're "out of line." "Don't even trip" equals "Don't worry about it." "With the quickness" is slang for quickly. "Give him his props" is "Give him credit." "Homeboy" is used for somebody from your hometown. "On the real" means true. "I got your back if you want to throw down" is analogous to "I will fight by your side against anybody."

"Parole punches" or "birthday punches" are code for when your buddies all hit you right before you go home or on your birthday. It's a whole different world inside the penitentiary.

Chapter 16:

Trying to Get Home

One of the most comforting words in the English language is "home." When you hear that word, doesn't it make you feel warm and safe inside? We all desire a belief in belonging to a particular locale. It doesn't matter where it is, or what it is. It may be the simplest of hovels, a shack or cabin in the woods, a grass hut, or a grandiose palace. The consistent thread is a haunt where you can hang your hat and feel at ease and relaxed, a sanctuary impervious to the stressors and ills of the world.

For many, the concept of a domicile includes having loved ones present. It may be your nuclear family (father, mother, spouse, brother, sister, son, or daughter). It might also include your extended family (grandparents, aunts, uncles, cousins, nieces, and nephews). In addition, you could have a friend or friends living at your pad. Whoever they are, you share a special bond with them because of their close proximity to you.

Some are alone, either by choice or by necessity. You possibly are a young adult who has left the nest already. Perhaps you have graduated from high school or college and wanted to venture out on your own to face the unforgiving globe with your new-found independence. You might be a widow or widower, continuing on without your life partner. Or you are still looking for Mr. or Mrs. Right. You could also be living alone because you enjoy the solitude, quietude, and freedom it offers.

On the trail to becoming an Eagle Scout, I participated in camp-outs in all kinds of venues, terrain, enclosures, weather, and seasons. No matter how much fun I had, or how many activities in which I was involved, or how many outdoor skills I learned, at its conclusion, I was always eager and ready to be homeward bound.

The notion of your residence can be expanded to include your neighborhood, hometown, home state, or home country. When I resided in SoCal, I spoke with pride about the state in which I grew up. In the same vein, while traveling throughout Europe, I took it as a badge of honor when I was recognized as an American. Even though it was a once-in-a-lifetime trip, I was exhilarated to be back on U.S. soil again.

A vacation away from your abode makes you appreciate your homestead even more. No matter how much utility you are experiencing on your junket, there's something alluring about returning to your old stomping grounds. Could it be that we have a genetic predisposition to nest like many animals do?

One of the most-loved movies of all-time, "The Wizard of Oz," is based on the premise of needing to return to your roots and holding them in high esteem. Dorothy went on a fantastic journey, made great friendships, and saw incredible sights. And yet, despite the glamour, all throughout the film she wanted to return to her beloved Kansas. She learned, for the first time, to appreciate her simple, mundane, bucolic life on the farm with Auntie Em. The gist of the film was that she had to leave and experience hardships in order to realize how valuable her household was.

When you are held against your will, the importance of your domestic lodging, liberty, and manumission means even more to you. They are transformed from mere sentiments to significant goals that greatly impact you. You cling onto that image tightly when life looks the bleakest. To truly cherish the worth of your dwelling, you need to empathize with those who tragically and involuntarily cannot reside at theirs. You might be lost, held in slavery, confined as a prisoner-of-war, or languishing in one of the world's jails or prisons.

Because of their spartan reality, inmates often fantasize or dream of abiding in their former, free habitation. About half my dreams are of the free world. Sigmund Freud would call that an escape mechanism. In order to hold onto hope, you have to believe you are extricable from your current surroundings. No matter how much time you have served or have yet to serve, the purport of your native shelter is sacred to all behind the wall. It is the epitome of Eden, the quintessential utopia. It is the symbol of emancipation and a lighthouse beacon to focus and concentrate on during the storm-tossed days of imprisonment.

Someday, I will be released from this dreadful hellhole. If I do survive this bit, I will joyfully and euphorically return to the house of my formative years. If I'm not alive to see it, at least my body will be buried in my beloved hometown. Either way, I'll be truly free, because like Judy Garland said, "There's no place like home."

Being in the slammer is like living in the Land of Oz: You see sights that boggle your imagination, you get acquainted with a few solid comrades, and you have to withstand an arduous ordeal teeming with malevolent fiends who want to inflict pain and suffering on you at every turn. There is One Supreme Being Who can grant every heart's desire (God, not the Wizard). Every convict's utmost hope lies in being released.

But there is a destination far more glorious ahead of us: our true, original habitat with our Heavenly Father. Everything else on earth pales in comparison to living someday with our Lord in Paradise. As spiritual beings, we have a predilection to return to our Creator and to live in eternal peace, harmony, grace, joy, mercy, and love. That denouement is our supreme, transcendent, unsurpassable home with Jesus.

Chapter 17:

Kindness is not Weakness

One of the most prevalent mantras and mind-sets in prison is that kindness is equivalent to weakness. For some reason, it seems to be a universal dogma in the penal system. Because of this apocryphal, fallacious point-of-view, institutions are teeming with callous, hardened convicts and wannabe tough guys. You don't dare show a scintilla of kindheartedness for fear you will be labeled "soft." If you ever receive that jacket, it's the kiss of death for you for the remainder of your bit.

How did this abhorrent perspective come

about? It probably originated as an offshoot of "the survival of the fittest" mentality. In order to demonstrate strength, you have to show effrontery and aggressiveness. Your senses are heightened and are in a constant mode of awareness and anticipation, regarding the protection of yourself and your possessions.

Some guys have told me, "I didn't come to prison to make friends," So, in order to not get burned, you don't consider anyone a chum; you don't want any pals. How sad. You don't know all the positive things that you're missing that stem from having interaction with others.

It doesn't make you a thug to intimidate, extort, or attack a timorous, vulnerable, weak, small, old, sickly, or frail dude. The men in here would contemn that despicable behavior, but it is still widespread. The "perp" will not get any "points" for doing such a cowardly, nefarious act. I freely assist the meek, underdogs, and outcasts because everyone has been on that side of the fence at one time or another.

There has to be a happy medium between

being a thoughtful, caring person and showing prospective predators that they shouldn't mess with you. You have to temper God's edict of loving your neighbor with the age-old inmate philosophy. What needs to shine through is that you are powerful–not feeble–by acting in a kind manner.

Jesus demonstrated His Almighty nature many times in the Bible, yet showed beneficence, forgiveness, and grace during His entire ministry, even during times of enormous stress. On the cross, He said in Luke 23:34, "Father, forgive them, for they do not know what they are doing." And to the repentant thief nine verses later, "I tell you the truth, today you will be with Me in paradise."

Our Savior's potency and puissance was beyond human comprehension, and so was His charity. Because He is my Paragon, I strive to live up to His impossible-to-reach standards. At significant personal cost and loss of social status, I have consistently displayed benefaction to many I've encountered, friend or foe.

Our Lord said in Matt. 25:35-36, 40, "For I was hungry and you gave me something to eat, I was thirsty and you gave me something to drink, I was a stranger and you invited me in, I needed clothes and you clothed me, I was sick and you looked after me, I was in prison and you came to visit me...I tell you the truth, whatsoever you did for one of the least of these brothers, you did it for Me."

You who have not shown benignity or mercy to me should remember that someday you will have a crisis, catastrophe, or ordeal and will look to others for much-needed compassion. What will happen then? What's in your heart today?

In Ephesians 4:32, St. Paul admonishes us to "be kind and compassionate to one another, forgiving each other, just as in Christ God forgave you." In 1 Thessalonians 5:15, it says, "Make sure nobody pays back wrong for wrong, but always try to be kind to each other." According to 2 Timothy 2:24, "The Lord's servant must not quarrel; instead, he must be kind to everyone."

Very rarely do you come across a staff person or a C.O. (corrections officer) who is warm-hearted. They seem like angels because they appear so incongruous with the surroundings by manifesting sympathy and understanding in this cauldron of evil.

As mentioned in chapter 1, life is all about showing love to one another and building relationships. The quality of your life is directly proportional to the quality of your connections with others. Being benevolent is a major component of that. Acts of selflessness are really just reciprocity without keeping score. It is not *quid pro quo,* where you only give as much as you've received.

Our Redeemer favors a giver filled with alacrity, with no underlying hidden or ulterior motives. While these dungeons may never become bastions of benignancy, if every felon softened his heart and showed humanity, there could be a revival of love and hope that would spread to all the nation's penitentiaries.

Chapter 18:

Mentally

The mental torture of being in prison or jail is a unique, profound experience. You don't know humiliation until you've walked in a pair of shackles, and nothing can prepare you for the unnerving sound of your cell door being slammed shut and locked. The feeling inside the wall is one of harsh, shell-shocked reality, with a large dose of lassitude, uneasiness, loneliness, and helplessness.

The pain of the loss of freedom is indescribable. Unless you've gone through it, it's impossible to comprehend the intense grief and horror that your mind undergoes as it tries to wrap itself around, and make sense of, your dire circumstances.

The opportunity cost of not being able to participate in society is enormous. You can drive yourself crazy by fixating on the absence of your loved ones, pets, hobbies, vacations, and high-tech gadgetry you are missing in the free world (a.k.a. "the block," "the world," or "the outs"). There is no Internet, laptops, cell phones, TiVo, DVR's, video games, phone cards, toll-free numbers, or MP3 players allowed. If you can't make the adjustment, the options are either having a nervous breakdown or committing suicide.

What accompanies this captivity? It is of paramount importance that you are completely dependent on others for your survival. If your sink doesn't function properly for an extended time, you could die of thirst. If you are not served nutritious food on a regular basis, you could meet your demise via malnutrition or starvation.

If you do not receive timely medical care, you can succumb to diseases or serious health conditions. If clean air doesn't come out of the vents, you could perish due to a lack of oxygen.

You are constantly at the mercy of your captors, which is a very sobering thought.

Adding to the already crazy, asylum-like atmosphere, there is rampant mental illness. Schizophrenia, bi-polar disorder, phobias, obsessive-compulsive disorder, depression, personality disorders, mood disorders, anxiety disorders, psychopaths, and sociopaths are ubiquitous. Every neurosis and psychosis known to man is represented in spades.

Many also have ADHD, which is marked by hyperactivity, being distracted easily, and having a short attention span while trying to concentrate. There is also a disproportionate amount of guys with traumatic brain injuries, which increases unpredictability. Everyone seems to have a significant defect of some sort.

How do you cope in this kind of environment? Your ordeal is made easier if you can get into a routine which makes life more predictable. Jotting down lists can help you stay organized. It's advantageous to be flexible and less rigid when plans go awry.

This is a fair and honest depiction about doing time in The Big House. As in chapter 15, I will try to paint for you the most accurate, ingenuous picture possible. I will begin with Corrections' philosophy, followed by specific policies. Along the way, I will intersperse some colloquialisms and their meanings.

You have to understand that the DOC is perfidious, maladroit, corrupt, and a hotbed for nepotism and cronyism. These sadists *never* have your best interests in mind and have no regard or respect for convicts whatsoever. By exuding total authority, they go out of their way to mess with their captives' already-fragile psyches.

Even in death, there is no dignity. Years ago, an offender was found ashen, bloated, and lifeless by a sentry. They handcuffed the corpse to the gurney as he was being wheeled away!

If they give you a direct order, no matter how inane, you will go to segregation if you don't follow it immediately. You have no choice but to go along with the program or face fearsome consequences. Everything is dictated to you: when to wake up, eat, stand up for count, have flag, lock in, and go to gym, yard, and work. No individual thinking is permitted.

The administration has an agenda of isolating you from the outside world and pitting inmates against each other in a diabolically twisted game of "divide and conquer." They organize mock elections in order to give you a feeling of fake empowerment. But, regardless of the outcome, they implement whatever they had in mind in the first place.

They make a concerted effort to be reticent and to minimize all communication. This equivocation keeps you in the dark because you don't know what is going on, or what to expect in the future. Obfuscation promotes confusion and chaos, which dissuades any unity.

You are forced to depend on unreliable rumors, guesses, and word-of-mouth speculations. Not only are many of these proven false and spurious, but there is no inclination from the higher-ups to want to improve in this area.

You can communicate with staff through

the use of "kites." They are called this because written requests used to be thrown down from the upper tiers, and thus resembled kites. They are yellow, lined paper, and you can broach any topic. They are often ignored or delegated for someone else to answer. The person you sent it to may never see it because it got intercepted by an underling.

You can't just write to anyone but must follow the chain of command up the ladder. If you keep running into roadblocks, you can file a grievance or even a lawsuit. Even though I've had ample reason to, I've never done it, mostly on account of the certain harsh retaliation expected.

The powers-that-be may invoke a new rule, but then not alert the population with a memo. All of a sudden, officers are enforcing this ordinance without giving any prior warning. Even if there is a notation, it rarely states any explanation or the rationale behind it.

They continually flout you by keeping you off-balance. They make you wait inordinately long before they decide to open up a locked door. They change the menu without telling anyone. They delay in calling you for a visit or an appointment. They won't even tell you if you have a pending engagement.

You are not able to plan ahead or schedule your day because you are constantly scrambling. It can get extremely frustrating knowing that they don't want you to be comfortable at all.

You have to wait in long lines to get chow, take a shower, go through metal detectors (they are everywhere), use the telephone, or receive canteen. You even have to wait an extra day to receive your mail (plus there's no mail on Saturdays). Patience is not my strong suit, but I've had to learn it the hard way.

The showers are communal, with no control over the temperature or speed of the spray. You have to hit a button on the showers and sinks every few seconds or they will shut off automatically. They don't want anyone to create a flood.

They try to "take you off your square" by conducting fire and tornado drills in the dark of night, or when it's really cold and rainy outside.

They conduct "emergency counts" whenever the power for the perimeter fence is lost or when there is ominous weather approaching. They do countless drills under the guise of training, contributing to the mental strain for the inhabitants.

When the guards do their rounds, they often shine their supernova-bright flashlights in your eyes, even when they can clearly see that your abode is already illuminated. This goes on every hour of every day, and is especially intrusive in the middle of the night when you are asleep.

They also bang loudly on your door if they don't see enough skin. They rattle your door and turn on "count lights" during their nightly rounds, and keep them on long after count has already cleared. That's either laziness or maliciousness.

The "flag" is the common day-space with rows of metal tables with connecting little, round chairs. It is called that because, in olden times, there was a U.S. flag present, and the floor was made of flagstone in that open area. Now, it means a free time when nothing mandatory is scheduled. You can play cards and board games, or just hang out and "chill." Each pod has 137 beds, and a miniscule courtyard where you can breathe fresh air and get a glimpse of nature.

You may opt to stay in your house if you are anti-social, afraid, abhor the cacophony, or just don't want to get "into the mix." However, you don't want to be labeled a "cave dweller," by virtue that it will appear you are scared or have something to hide.

The noise level is so extreme that, if you've done a significant amount of time, you'll suffer some hearing loss. Contributors to the dissonance are dominoes being slammed on the tables, guys screaming at the top of their lungs, music blaring from TV's and radios, coppers shouting orders, and the deafening PA system paging people.

Inexplicably, the screws choose not to enforce the noise regulation. It makes it impossible to get any quality sleep, or concentrate on reading, writing, or the task at hand. You never get used to it, and it causes a huge amount of tension and stress. There are two stand-up counts each day (some venues have three). They ring a bell and announce it at 10:30 a.m. and 9:20 p.m. You have to stand by your door window with the light on and your I.D. in hand until the C.O. acknowledges you. It can be a fairly long wait.

The decision-makers firmly believe in the widely-discredited theory of punishing everyone for the inappropriate actions of a few (or the one). To illustrate, if a tough beats up a cop, the perp will be sent to the dungeons. The rest of the unit will be punished by being locked down for an indefinite period of time, even though no other party was involved. That kind of idiocy inflames a lot of resentment and indignation.

By the same token, if a criminal misuses an object due to his own selfishness, they will strip that item from everyone, even if it is innocuous and 99% of the residents were using it for its intended purpose.

At a previous institution, some knucklehead boiled honey in a microwave and threw it in another guy's face. It was very scary and very stupid. Because of this senseless act, they took away all the microwaves for a long duration.

One of their most burdensome edicts says that you have to put all of your possessions (for some, that means everything you own) into two diminutive plastic bins and jettison anything that doesn't fit. They can order this done at any time, so you have to always be prepared. Your bland state clothing (in limited colors only) takes up nearly one by itself.

That means your shoes, hygiene, canteen, electronics, plastic pitchers, photo albums, paperwork, books, magazines, newspapers, keepsakes, medications, and everything else has to fit into one tiny tub. There is a bare-bones limit on each article. Why would they place a ceiling on how many personal photographs you can have? That seems unnecessary.

In addition, nothing can be altered, or it will be confiscated. Yet, you can check out a small scissors from the bubble (a glass-enclosed office where rapscallions are forbidden) and buy a sewing kit. Using either will automatically modify anything on which they are used.

The authorities consistently deprive prisoners of a laundry list of lares and penates by trotting out generic excuses like "It's a fire hazard" or "It jeopardizes security." These umbrella phrases give them supreme power to deny anything. Things taken away by this convoluted logic include plastic coolers, homemade stuff received in the mail, paper bags, paper towels, anything on your walls outside of a tiny square, et al.

In order to expedite any searches, they decided that everything needed to be clear in color for ease in inspection. Anything in a different color must be sent out. They might "grandfather in" a belonging, but then later place a "sunset date" on it and take it away.

If I listed all the personal effects they've taken away during the last quarter-century, it would make *War and Peace* look like a pamphlet. Some notables include: a rug for the floor, seven pairs of personal pants and shirts, outside-vendor shoes, oscillating fans, gold watches, necklaces, and wedding rings with stones in them, headphones, black radios, a variety of foods, unlimited books and periodicals, two Christmas boxes from the outs (totaling 25 lbs), cigarettes and other tobacco products, "R"-rated movies, the ability to crank open the window, restaurant food, and a myriad of goods from businesses in the free world.

The Department has a monopoly on food, clothing, electronics, toiletries, and shoes. Very rarely are you afforded an opportunity to buy anything from an outside, prior-approved concern.

Contraband is anything on your person or in your domicile that is not approved: paper clips, gum, money, nude pictures, gambling paraphernalia, illegal drugs, hooch (homemade alcohol), tobacco, escape materials, evidence of running a store (lending canteen items at a 50% mark-up), and anything that has been purloined.

The turnkeys conduct room searches and hooch checks haphazardly. (You can always hear them approaching due to the jangling of their keys.) You are ordered to leave, then one or more jailers enter and proceed to tear apart your dwelling and rifle through your chattel.

If everything is not immaculate, they will ask you pointed, suspicious questions. Sometimes, they will even seize doodads without telling you. The aftermath looks like a tornado tore through, and you feel victimized by the burglary.

Every so often, there will either be a unit or an institution-wide lockdown. The impetus can be random or causative. You and your bunkie are confined until it is over, which can be one day to several weeks. You are strip-searched, handcuffed, and taken away to a holding area, while your home is thoroughly searched.

During a modified lockdown, you are shut in all day so that your complex flatfeet can help conduct a search in another complex.

If you break any rule, you will be punished either informally (where you receive "LOP" [Loss of Privileges], or "privs") or formally (where you go to the hole). Both types of infractions involve a write-up. They can also put you on "IRR" (Idle Room Restriction), where you can't leave your quarters for 24 hours while they conduct an investigation.

LOP (one hour of flag: no phone calls, yard, or gym) is given progressively for a plethora of offenses: not wearing your ID or going shirtless outside of your household, having or smuggling innocuous contraband, running (except during yard or gym), not standing during count, pushing your duress button frivolously, covering your window or vents, hanging a blanket for privacy while defecating (plus pay a fine for the cost of a new one), having an excess of clothes or linen/pillows/blankets, sporting fresh tattoos, getting mouthy with the employees, shadowboxing, g-ratting, horseplay, etc.

Formal discipline would apply when being involved in a fight (even if you weren't the aggressor or didn't fight back), having a weapon, threatening someone (verbally, on the phone, or through the mail), setting off a metal detector (even if the culprit is a pair of glasses, fingernail clipper, or candy wrapper!), being in an unauthorized area, misrepresenting yourself, masturbating, sexually assaulting anyone, attempting to commit suicide, committing suicide (how would they punish that?), possessing escape plans or hooch, plus numerous others.

Randomly, you might get called for a "UA," or Urine Analysis test. You are strip-searched in a bathroom and scrutinized as you produce a sample. If you can't provide one within two hours, or if it comes back dirty, they will haul you to segregation. You may be brought to a holding area called a "bullpen," which gives the connotation of preparing for a big event. It is most notably a large space in a courthouse that is packed to the gills with men waiting to go into the courtroom.

If the alarm on the officers' radios goes off, it signifies an "ICS" (Incident Command System) is occurring, and the "goon squad," a small contingent of police armed with mace and other weapons, springs into action. They break up altercations, assist with medical calls, and escort hooligans, cuffed in the back, to "seg." All felon movement comes to a halt until the "all-clear" has been given.

The ruffians in hot water are then placed in the middle of a crude hovel, adorned with only a bed, sink, and toilet. The squad surrounds you and carries out an exhaustive body cavity search. Your clothes are snatched, and you are given heavily-used, threadbare ones instead.

You have no access to any of your holdings in the hole and meals are delivered through a book pass. After being there a while, you can get up to one hour of flag time a day and a shower every three days. You can't relax with the unrelenting screaming all day and night, which stems from both anger and boredom.

The bright light is mandatorily on 18 hours a day which, along with the aforementioned stentorian conditions, makes getting any quality sleep a nightmare. All of your visits are transmitted over a T.V. monitor, instead of being face-to-face. Anytime you go anywhere (such as health services), you are chained up.

You lose a great deal when you go to solitary. You lose your job, cellie, bunk, paycheck, and self-esteem. While you are wasting away, the property people are eagerly sifting through all your junk with a fine-toothed comb, looking for anything illicit and jocosely divesting you of your gear. You are violated yet again.

Then, to make matters worse, you are subject to the two footlocker canon before they'll let you leave property. Anything extraneous has to be discarded, donated, or sent out (for an exorbitant fee).

If a serious transgression occurs, you will have a hearing before a disciplinary board in "Due Process" (which is anything but). In this "kangaroo court," you're presumed to be guilty before the proceedings even start.

You get to tell your side of the story and call witnesses, but with the opposition being judge, jury, prosecutor, and executioner, the fight isn't a fair one. Behind the scenes, the "OSI" (Office of Special Investigations) crew is constantly monitoring everyone, hoping to break open a big case.

The job situation is horrendous. For 1,000 dudes, there might be approximately 400 slots. Depending on your status, you may not have a choice of positions, but just assigned one.

Absolutely no benefits are given. There are no paid holidays (you are restricted to your cell in order to save the state money), no paid vacation, and no paid sick days.

Not only that, you will be fired if you take three unapproved absences during a 6-month period, miss five consecutive working days for *any* reason, or violate a statute. The most insane decree is that you can't stay in the same assignment for longer than four contiguous years.

You would think they would encourage you to find your niche, find something you're good at, and experience a scintilla of satisfaction, accomplishment, and fulfillment. But, no! They would rather pull the rug out from under you, disrupt your life, and enervate any initiative or incentive.

You have to be at work by 6:30 a.m. That's an early start to the day. The wages are abysmal, as evidenced by some making as little as 12.5 cents per hour. It definitely has a sweatshop atmosphere. One year, my full-time job paid me, before deductions, a cool $491. Some of you readers make that in one day!

They thieve 5% from your gross pay for a slush fund they call "aid to victims." If you're lucky enough to get one of the few interstate posts, you will then be rewarded by having 80% taken out for federal taxes, state taxes, and "cost of confinement."

With their greedy, grubby hands, the State also takes 10% of any monies sent in to you. They dutifully charge a $5.00 co-pay for every time you see the dentist (every other year), eye doctor (every other year), doctor, or nurse (via sick-call).

The canteen is marked-up an average of 65% from regular wholesale prices, and there are no sales or coupons. This causes undue financial hardship. As you can see, they are nickel-and-diming to the extreme, while making a boatload of cash off the misery of others.

If you are not employed, you must live in a "SHU", (Special Housing Unit). There, you are imprisoned with your roomie (you better hope you don't have a bad one) 23 hours/day, with limited yard and gym time. The adage is fondly referred to as "no work, no play." To make matters worse, you're locked outside of your box for the last 45 minutes of flag, and the microwave is off-limits.

Penitentiary life is Bizzaro World–everything appears backwards and upside-down. I wasn't cynical before incarceration, but now I have trust issues, brought about by being burned repeatedly by traitors and backstabbers. However, I continue to be sanguine and put my trust and faith in the Lord Jesus Christ, despite the profusion of bunkum I am subjected to on a daily basis.

Chapter 19:

Physically

Being incarcerated can exact a prodigious toll on you physically. If you are not careful, you can easily die prematurely behind the wall by reaching your nadir, and giving up by letting yourself go. This is an easy thing to do, considering the tremendous emotional and psychological burden you must carry on a daily basis.

In a physical sense, being imprisoned is extremely grueling. It takes a little bit out of you every day, and over a long time, this constant erosion inexorably makes a massive, negative impact on your health and well-being.

The adverse consequences of stress

produce torpor and wear down your body over the long haul. You might become hirsute, or stop exercising, eating right, and getting enough rest. In extreme cases, you might capitulate and decide basic hygiene is no longer necessary. You can quickly identify these morose, tormented souls by the emanations of severe B.O. on account of not showering regularly. They have filthy clothes on, and shuffle around lethargically in profound sadness with blank, vacant eyes.

The fall-out from feeling undue pressure may cause overeating (for comfort), insomnia, anxiety, ulcers, and nervous disorders. The effects are exacerbated when you have little or no hope of ever getting out again. You may come in as a "lean, mean, fighting machine," but oftentimes you leave as something quite different.

What is the origin of all this tension? First, there is the continual, ceaseless, perpetual trepidation and fear of being in mortal danger. It's no secret that prison is a hotbed for spurious rumors and ferocious acts. Inmates routinely fight each other, guards, and other staff members.

You can never let your guard down for one second because the potential for vehemence is always present. You never know when some maniac will jump you from behind and sucker-punch you when you're not looking, for no reason at all.

Certain words will spark a fight instantly. For examples, if someone calls you a "bitch" or "punk," there will automatically be an intense eruption. Because, if you don't handle business right then and there, you will be labeled those words, and carry around that heavy jacket for the rest of your bit. If you are planning on mixing it up with somebody "on sight," that means that whenever you spot that person, you will instantly attack them, no matter the circumstances or the venue.

Getting enough quality sleep is extremely elusive. There is nothing available that is soporific. What with the never-ending P.A. announcements blaring, the excessive shouting by unruly scofflaws, and your cellie banging around the room, life can be downright unbearable. The count light is on all night, and there has been a

7:00 a.m. stand-up count, which prevents anyone from sleeping in. You never seem to get caught up on your sleep debt. All of this contributes to your ongoing suffering.

The cells are ice-cold year-round, and there's no way to increase the heat. You are given only two threadbare blankets for a modicum of warmth. During the winter, you are provided a light jacket, but no scarves, no gloves, and no masks. Strangely, the architects designed the campus so that the buildings are not connected. Therefore, you have to walk a great distance in the freezing cold (during the winter months) to go anywhere.

There are generally two schools of thought in regards to training. One group is indefatigable and germinates sinew obsessively, and the other has no compulsion whatsoever for it and is comprised of sedentary couch-potatoes. You get one hour of gym and one hour of yard per day, six days a week, and the courtyard is diminutive, with no equipment available.

The indomitable "go-getters" are sedulous,

and spend an inordinate amount of time lifting weights, walking/jogging around the track or on the treadmill, playing sports, and being mindful of improving their fitness. I fall into this category, but I'm not as gung-ho and tenacious as I ought to be.

You can be overboard on your routine and sacrifice all other aspects of living in population (e.g. religious services, schoolwork, and making/improving social contacts), as well as on the outside (e.g. family, friends, and relatives). You need to strike a balance and find a happy medium encompassing the many different strata of options you have at your disposal.

Granted, if you are going to err on any one side, definitely let it be on the side of motility. The many benefits of that course has been proven repeatedly through empirical evidence. Besides keeping you hale and hearty, exertion is efficacious in giving you a natural high through the release of endorphins at the conclusion of a heightened workout.

Even though it provides innumerable

benefits, it can get prosaic, and you should still practice it in measured sessions. Working out too often or too intensely, or using the same muscle groups too repetitively, can cause injuries, unhealthy imbalances, and an abeyance on activities.

On the other side of the coin, if you become a sluggard and phlegmatic, only bad things can happen. Every part of your anatomy will be adversely affected by the desuetude of movement. Through extrapolation, your strength will atrophy, your blood pressure will increase, your lung capacity will decrease, your cardiovascular system will become less efficient, and your chances for stroke, cancer, heart attack, and diabetes will skyrocket. You will also tire more easily.

If all of that is not reason enough to stay fit, the accompanying weight gain will cause your self-esteem to plummet, and you will become a target for ostracization. Society teaches at a young age that being fat is synonymous with laziness, sloth, gluttony, and lack of willpower and self-control. Our culture puts a premium on thinness as the standard for beauty. If you are turgid, you may be inveighed a fulsome, social pariah and be blackballed from participation in social activities.

The overweight person may simply have slow metabolism or be genetically predisposed to corpulence. Name-calling and tearing down others have no place in interpersonal relationships. We should treat each other with love, respect, consideration, and compassion at all times. Jesus announced this Golden Rule in Matthew 19:19, "Love your neighbor as yourself." We should support one another instead of pointing fingers and criticizing. Paul said in Romans 14:13, "Therefore let us stop passing judgment on one another."

Another important factor is your diet. Eating right is critical in attaining and maintaining equilibrium in terms of vitamins, minerals, and nutrients. By remembering the food pyramid, you know how many helpings of fruit, vegetables, carbohydrates, dairy, and protein you should have each day.

The conundrum, however, is how do you

eat salutary in the pen? It is next to impossible. It is easy to grouse when there is only a scant amount of nutritious sustenance available. Only the very minimum requirements are served, and the caliber leaves much to be desired.

For example, the vegetables are often overcooked into a mushy paste with most of the nourishment boiled out. You receive ground-up turkey instead of ground-up beef because it is a cheaper alternative. Also, there has been no pork served for the last 20 years on account of the protests from the Muslims. The grub is extremely vapid by virtue of no herbs or spices being used. All you have available to use is salt and pepper.

The menu is on a five-week cycle, so there is a great deal of repetition and very little variety. There is a strong emphasis on high-caloric, processed edibles laden with gratuitous amounts of fat, sugar, cholesterol, and preservatives. Salt, which increases hypertension, is ubiquitous in most of the products. One decent alimentary vehicle, a salad bar, was discontinued. In short, the cuisine is bottom-of-the-barrel, unhealthy (boxes in the kitchen have been found to say "unfit for human consumption," or they are on a recall list), pre-packaged, cheap, old (past the expiration date), and poorly prepared.

The chow hall is huge, with rows of long, stainless steel tables, with little, round, metal seats on both sides, spaced closely together. You have zero elbow room, and you feel like livestock eating at a trough all at the same time.

You have to prepare your own meals because they just throw the food ingredients on your tray. You arrive as a unit, and you leave as a unit. You have to scarf down your meal because you might only get 10-15 minutes to eat. You are subject to petty rules like "stay inside the red line." If you delay in leaving, you will get written-up.

The hygiene of the preparers, handlers, and servers is extremely suspect. There have been instances of kitchen workers putting pubic hairs, boogers, mucous, urine, and semen into the victuals. Pleasant thought, huh? You are at the mercy of a private food company only interested in its bottom line. It does not care one iota about your welfare. The grade of the eats available in the canteen is every bit as bad as that served in the cafeteria. They are generic and substandard without a name-brand as far as the eye can see. In addition, you cannot order any outside foodstuffs.

The Health Services department is so antiquated and low-tech that you half-way expect to see a jar of leeches when you enter the doctor's office. It is medicine from the Middle Ages. You have to be on a waiting list for two years in order to see a dentist or an optometrist because they visit so rarely.

They don't want to perform any procedure or give you medications because that costs them money, so they stymie you at every turn. They pooh-pooh you and blow you off dismissively if you bring up any medical concern. They instruct you to take two ibuprofen tablets for every imaginable malady, in keeping with their frugalness. You have to self-diagnose and self-treat anything that comes your way. Incidentally, I'm one of the few convicts who has all of my teeth and no tattoos.

It's so easy to get run-down and stay that

way. At work, you get *no* breaks whatsoever, paid or not (unless you count using one of the three toilets available for 200 people). You cannot eat or drink at the shop, and it is all manual labor. This leads to even more fatigue. As the saying goes, "I'm sick and tired of being sick and tired."

As you can see, staying sound and fit as a fiddle behind bars is very challenging because of the many obstacles you must overcome. It is very easy to become complacent because of the ever-present feelings of hopelessness and depression. What is the incentive to do all the hard work for optimum fitness when you might never be free again?

Even the staunchest advocates of staying salubrious have trouble sticking with their programs in this kind of caustic environment. All you can do is try your very best to be active, consume, in temperance, a balanced diet, and try to eliminate as much strain from your life as you can. By doing that, it can only help in the long run, and in all other aspects of your life as well.

The important thing to remember is that

you are only given one mortal shell. You should take great care of it and respond to its needs. The Apostle Paul said in his first letter to the Corinthians 6:19, “Your body is a temple of the Holy Spirit...You are not your own.” How you treat it could ultimately determine your future wellness and longevity.

Chapter 20:

EMOTIONALLY

The range and intensity of emotions that you experience while being incarcerated is quite prodigious. Often, they change on a dime without any warning. Having to cope with life-threatening circumstances, and staying cool under enormous pressure, is something that you have to learn in order to survive.

If you ever lose control of your sensibilities, the consequences can be lethal. Most debacles result when you let "bad feelings" fester, and they create a life of their own. If you have a quick temper, and most do, you will spend a lot of your sentence sitting in the hole.

Conditions in segregation depend greatly

upon in which state you are doing time. Some are on the extreme side, like stripping you of all of your clothing, being in complete darkness, and having a dirt floor with a hole in the middle for toilet facilities. It's only you and the four bare walls. You have to be emotively strong to make it through those circumstances unscathed. If you get combative, you could get strapped to a surfboard naked for hours at a time.

To compound matters, the cell is kept ice-cold, and you would get barely-survivable rations of food. The sensory deprivation takes its toll on you psychologically and emotionally. It's a basic human need to connect to others and interact with them. These surroundings are designed to remind you "who is really in charge."

The DOC strongly discourages you to have any intimacy with your family, relatives, and friends. For example, when you get a visitor, you are only allowed a short hug at the beginning and end of your visit. You can't even kiss your girlfriend or wife on the lips at any time (only a kiss on the cheek is acceptable during your hug). In addition, you have to sit across from your visitor and can make no contact whatsoever while seated.

The friends you make in the joint are transitory because they come and go like a revolving door. It makes you feel lachrymose seeing your buddy uprooted and not knowing if you'll ever see him again.

I have a problem with anyone who lowers my quality of life and makes everyday living more arduous. Because of the mountain of pain and suffering I've endured all of these years, as a defense mechanism and survival technique, I have become numb and calloused emotionally in order to protect myself from further injury. It's my way of coping with the magnitude of anguish that I feel.

In many ways, I died 25 years ago. It makes me very lugubrious to no longer be a part of society. I'm like a ghost–just observing and not participating. As time goes by, my emotional connections become fewer and fewer.

Contrary to popular belief, you can experience sentimental highs in the pen. They are rare, so they are savored and cherished. What can bring about this temporary euphoria?

You could have an awesome drop-in from a loved one. You get to spend some quality time with someone who cares for you (plus you get to get out of the cell hall). You might even find yourself smiling or laughing during your visitation.

You could also get an upper by receiving a card or letter from a special person. When you pull mail out of your mailbox, you often hear, "Someone loves you."

I have been exceedingly blessed to have many precious people in my life who have fervently supported me. Each person is special to me in their own unique way. It is overwhelming to think about the heartfelt, moving words contained in their missives, not to mention the sincere prayers raised to the Almighty to intercede on my behalf. They have, with their busy schedules, tirelessly devoted and sacrificed their time, energy, love, talents, and finances to visit, write, talk on the phone, and pray for me. It makes life so much more bearable and mitigates my negative milieu.

These caring individuals are truly children of our Heavenly Father. Compassion, kindness, warmth, and understanding are God's love in action.

Words don't do justice for the gratitude and appreciation in my heart for all of these wonderful, generous people. Anything done to help my cause is acknowledged and remembered. More importantly, each unselfish act is recorded in the Almighty's heavenly books. By doing these deeds of altruism, our Lord countenances when He sees His Word become fruitful.

Chapter 21:

Socially

There is an unwritten Convict Code of Conduct that serves as a broad template for all prisoners to follow. These guidelines are not suggestions, but are hard-and-fast rules rigidly enforced by the hard-cores. The paramount edict is “Don’t squeal.” If you rat on someone in a police report or in a court of law, you violate this sacred cow.

By the same token, if you volunteer information to the detriment of a fellow inmate in order to gain favor from the outside cops, the district attorney, or the penitentiary guards, you will be labeled as a snitch for the rest of your life. The cowardly drop surreptitious, anonymous kites to the authorities.

If you are found out, you will, at best, be a permanent social outcast. At worst, you could get pummeled repeatedly or even killed. By committing this transgression, you put the entire population at risk. If you have the audacity to tell on another right in front of him, it's called "dry snitching."

Your name is pellucid because it is written above your cell door and you have to wear an I.D. on your shirt wherever you go. Another tenet to be followed is "Don't get into other people's business." It is considered rude and a blatant invasion of privacy. That means to not ask others about their personal lives or their families. Obviously, for safety reasons, you don't want extraordinarily violent criminals to know the names of your loved ones or where they reside. You can't fully trust anyone behind the wall, even your "friends."

Also, you should never ask anyone about their criminal case. That knowledge could lead to all kinds of ostracization and extortion ramifications. Even though it's nobody else's concern, dudes still look up others' cases on the

Internet or in the Law Library.

Gossiping can be destructive anywhere, but it can be downright deadly in the joint. If you are the object of derision, it is practically impossible to repair your stained reputation. You don't want others talking about you behind your back, especially if it is scurrilous or defamatory. You are risking your physical well-being by whispering about others. I like to know the current scuttlebutt, but not at the expense of my fellow man.

How you carry yourself has a direct correlation to how you're viewed. If you diligently follow the Convict Code and treat others with respect, you will be known as a "stand-up guy." Of course, the respect you give abruptly ends if you are disrespected. It has to be a two-way street.

I'm polite and courteous to the guards and staff as long as they don't go out of their way (or outside of their job descriptions) to make my life harder than it already is. Guards need to be fair, humane, and consistent.

You may have a sterling reputation, but if

you move to a new venue where they don't know you, you have to prove yourself all over again. There will always be fools who will test you to see of what you are made. The best thing to do is be steadfast and put each situation in God's hands.

I made a conscious effort to be warm and friendly to everybody and am careful not to ruffle any feathers. The last thing you want to do is make an enemy. Felons in the pen hold grudges forever and will do everything in their power to inflict pain on you in countless ways.

Everyone seems to have a "hustle" or scam. You may be selling meds, tattooing, running a store, drawing greeting cards, selling meals you prepare, marketing legal advice, or gambling on cards, chess, or sports.

Most inmates have very limited social skills. They demonstrate sparse decorum or tact, and blurt out whatever is on their minds without filtering the content first. They tend to be frank, direct, crude, and ribald.

There is a clear hierarchy in prison. Fair or not, you can command significant respect or be the recipient of great disparagement. Your status is derived from the nature of your case and how you carry yourself and interact with others.

At the very bottom of the barrel are the informants because they represent a perpetual threat and can never be trusted. If you are willing to testify in court against another offender for a reduced sentence of your own, you're liable to do anything for your own personal gain.

The next lowest rung is reserved for child molesters. Children are the most vulnerable victims and are often emotionally scarred for life by the abuse. The next step up are the rapists. They are looked down upon because the general feeling is that a "real man" should not have to use force in order to have sexual contact with a woman.

If you are on any of the bottom three levels, you will be subjected to frequent badgering, myriad invectives, and many physical confrontations. Friends and acquaintances will suddenly stop talking to you when they find out the truth, and you will live in constant fear because there is no place to hide.

The rest of the cases are thrown together in a big amalgamation. The only exception is murder, which occupies the top-tier social status. The reasoning is that if you took a life once, you are most likely willing to do it again, without hesitation. That makes you a man to be feared.

A subset of this niche, the cop killer, is at the very top of the ladder. This is due to the prevailing perception that all police are the enemy, and thus need to be eliminated. These assassins aren't exactly the favorites of the guards or staff.

Street gangs have infiltrated the nation's jails and prisons and have proliferated and thrived through coercion, force, fear, and extreme truculence. They are predominately broken down by race, with a few exceptions. Each one is ruled by a rigid hierarchy and a set of written by-laws. There is a designated leader for each organization on a national, state, institution, and cell hall basis. The top dog is called the "shot-caller." Under him are his lieutenants, followed by the rest of the rank-and-file.

They are always out recruiting for newbies because there is strength in numbers. If you want to pledge, you first have to have a case that is considered "acceptable." After you are an official plebe, you will have to endure a long probation period. You will be sent on "missions" (a physical attack on another person) in order to prove your toughness.

You also become the group's lackey, which means you might have to store hooch in your room, do calisthenics on-call, be a "mule" and smuggle items, or perform any other whim your brothers might dream up. You will probably have to run through a gauntlet where the rest of the mob get to line up and punch you, and you aren't allowed to hit back. The concept of "blood in, blood out" means that you have to shed blood in order to gain full membership or if you ever want to leave the gang.

Each pack has its own colors, complete with wearing dog tags around their necks (the institution clothes are drab in color so as not to identify with any one coterie). They also have their own unique signs, handshakes, and tattoos (called patches).

You can always identify a gangbanger because they are supposed to wear tennis shoes to the shower. This is to give them better traction than flip-flops in case a fight breaks out. They have to show their leaders any kites before they can mail them, and they receive "care packages" from other members should they end up in the hole. An old gang member can retire and receive the venerable label "O.G." for Original Gangster.

They make their money by extortion and by offering protection. Extortion, or "kicking in," is when they make a list of canteen items and drop it off to a victim who comes across as weak or in on a "bad" case. If the "vic" doesn't deliver the merchandise on canteen day, several toughs will knock him around. When the "gump" returns to population, they will continue to beat him senseless until he pays up on a continual basis.

Protection is different in the sense that it is voluntary, at least at the outset. You may be having trouble with an individual or ring and need some help. You will remunerate a store list on a regular basis as well, even after you no longer want/need protection anymore. The circle will deal with anyone who messes with their "client."

If a "cliqued-in" thug, client, or anyone else acts "out of pocket," the syndicate can fine them for what they perceive as a *faux paus.* The gangsters exert a great deal of power and control over the administration and guards because they know that the "big-ballers" can either keep the peace or "jump things off." They kowtow to them and give them many special favors and plenty of latitude.

If you get too scared, you can "check-in" to protective custody (P.C.). You will be separated from the mainline population in administrative segregation (ad-seg). There is great stigma attached to this move though because it is perceived as recreancy. And you can't stay in it forever; it is only temporary.

Penal institutions are some of the most racist places on earth. It seems like every aspect is demarcated by ethnic groups: sports teams, telephones, tables on the flag and in the mess hall, religious groups, and social groups. The crews even bus their meal trays together to show solidarity. I try to treat all people with kindness, respect, and compassion, no matter what their complexion, creed, religion, gender, sexual orientation, or national origin is.

You can get into serious trouble just for conversing with someone who is another color, as there is rampant racial hatred. You might refuse to room with a person from another race or experience grave problems if you have no choice. You naturally gravitate toward others like yourself because you share a commonality or bond with them. It is also for safety reasons, because if a race war "jumps off," you would rely on each other to "have your back." If you fail to "get down," you could get jumped by your own kind.

One of the most unnatural environments is where two grown men have to share a living space the size of an average bathroom. You have just one small shelf and desk to put all of your possessions, so it can get very cluttered and confining. I've had over thirty cellies, and they have all had their own idiosyncrasies and foibles.

For example, some want you to flush while you are urinating so they don't have to hear it. Many think it's preferable to brush your teeth in the toilet. Who does that at home? You sometimes get total slobs who have no concept of hygiene (overripe B.O.) or cleanliness (like not washing their dishes or clothes for an extended period). Occasionally, you even have to cope with otherworldly flatulence emanations.

Often, there is a power struggle for control of the dwelling. He might disrespect you by cranking up his T.V. or radio, or by singing or laughing loudly even when you're trying to sleep. He might be a hermit and rarely leave the domicile. A fair amount become institutionalized, which means they no longer think for themselves but blindly follow whatever the DOC has programmed them to do.

Your roomie could be a loud, chronic snorer or you might be kept awake by the late-night flickering of his T.V. screen. He could invite his buddies over and disturb your peace by talking to them in the doorway. There's a chance he could steal your property, intimidate, threaten, or extort you. If he is homosexual, or in order to show dominance (being "prison gay"), he might try to rape or molest you. If you aren't compatible, then you have to walk on eggshells all the time.

Society despises ex-cons and it places them under a microscope with the utmost scrutiny. The social ramifications and stigma of being incarcerated will follow you wherever you go for the rest of your life. Anyone can Google you and find out your entire criminal history. That stain on your record will make finding a girlfriend/wife or a decent job all the more difficult. No matter if you were a captain of industry, doctor, lawyer, teacher, accountant, or in any other profession before you were arrested, you will become a pariah and a *persona non grata* afterwards.

Chapter 22:

Spiritually

There is a palpable undercurrent of turpitude in penal institutions via imprecation, like a bubbling cauldron of wickedness waiting to explode. There is a constant, malevolent pall over a penitentiary, and it seems like demons and every unclean spirit take up residence there. They permeate and infiltrate every square inch of the facility. It is Party Central for the Devil, the bane of man, and his cohorts. It makes the atmosphere hostile, caustic, and toxic.

It should come as no surprise in our dissolute society that there has been an accelerated rise in profanity, crudeness, vulgarity, ribald humor, and untoward behavior (as discussed in Chapter 2). Spiritual warfare seems to be increasing in its intensity, both inside and outside the joint. Maybe it's because Satan knows that his time is short, and he is becoming more desperate with our Messiah returning soon to reclaim His kingdom on earth.

The Holy Spirit, our Comforter, is the part of the Triune God Who lives in the heart of a Christian believer. We can't have any faith without Him, and He helps us in times of need to make the right decisions.

The Holy Spirit is mentioned often in the New Testament. Jesus said in John 16:13-14, "When He, the Spirit of Truth, comes, He will guide you into all truth. He will bring glory to Me." Paul wrote in Chapter 8 in his letter to the Roman (v.9) "If anyone does not have the Spirit of Christ, he does not belong to Christ." (v.14) "Those who are led by the Spirit of God are sons of God." (v.17) "Now if we are children, then we are heirs–heirs of God and co-heirs with Christ... that we may also share in His glory." (v.26,27)

"The Spirit helps us in our weakness. We do not know what we ought to pray for, but the Spirit Himself intercedes for...the saints in accordance with God's will."

In 1 Corinthians 2:12, 13 it is written, "We have...received...the Spirit Who is from God, that we may understand what God has freely given us...in words taught by the Spirit, expressing spiritual truths in spiritual words." In Galatians 6:8 we find, "The one who sows to please the Spirit, from the Spirit will reap eternal life."

You may not have been spiritually-minded before your time behind bars, but through the experience, you may be drawn to the Almighty. Yes, many cynics will call it "jailhouse religion," a pejorative term meaning you only found the Lord because you have reached rock-bottom. It's true that you reach out to a higher power when your life is in the crapper, and you have nowhere else in which to turn.

With incredible pain and suffering, comes prodigious soul-searching and introspection. You start asking yourself recondite, philosophical questions such as, "Why was I put on this earth, and by whom? What is my purpose, and my hopes, dreams, and goals for the future?" Maybe you've never plumbed the depths of your own psyche before, but being in a life-or-death predicament will cause you to contemplate and ruminate.

You might realize that the circumstances you find yourself in are beyond your control. You may be having a difficult time dealing with your situation and coping with the gravity of consequences. You reach out to your only hope, after having tried everything else: God. Scoffers will call you insincere because you didn't have time for the King of Kings before your incarceration.

But our inscrutable Heavenly Father draws His children to Himself in many different ways, and being locked-up is but one avenue to our Creator. He is famous for turning a negative station in life into a positive one.

One welcomed exception to the racial divide is during chapel services and Bible studies. There, the color of the skin is unimportant, only the color of your heart. Black, white, red, yellow, and brown races come together as brothers-in-Christ to worship and praise the Supreme Being. Jesus is "color-blind," and so should we be also.

Chapter 23:

HIS PLAN

What is our Heavenly Father's Will or Plan? It is impossible for any of us to discern the Mind of the Almighty. Isaiah 55:8 says, "'For My thoughts are not your thoughts, neither are your ways My ways,' says the Lord." However, the Bible does provide us with some clues.

His Plan is always perfect and He always knows best, even if we don't understand or agree with it. The Divine One is sovereign and in complete control over the entire universe. He is awesome, majestic, absolute, and all-powerful. He is not limited by man-made constraints. Nothing happens unless He ordains or allows it.

James 4:15 has this to say, "You ought to say, 'If it is the Lord's Will, we will live and do this or that.' " We should be malleable and tractable, open to receiving direction from Him. After many years, I have finally learned to submit and acquiesce to the King of Kings in all matters, in all ways, at all times, and in all places. He is the Captain of my ship and Driver of my car.

A popular phrase right now is, "Let go and let God." We need to put our complete faith and trust in Him. In 1 John 5:14 it is written, "If we ask anything according to His Will, He hears us." Our finite minds cannot grasp the scope of His infinity or His vastness. We are constantly learning about the sheer immensity of the universe and all the mysteries it holds. In addition, what about the complex intricacies that make up the human body? The beauty, order, and balance of the cosmos provides unmistakable evidence that it was all created by a higher power. If we look around, we realize how small we really are in relation to all of creation, and how the Lord of Hosts has had a hand in everything.

As a species, we are conceited and arrogant, and often broach His Will for us. We think we have great significance and know best because of our intelligence, and we remain stubborn, froward, and refractory.

But, when we remember our proper place in the grand scheme of things, we will have the appropriate humility, respect, fear, and reverence for our Creator. He will chastise, discipline, and test His children so that we may become the mature believers that He wants us to be.

The Master wants the very best for mankind (we are made in His image, after all), and He wants everyone to be saved from damnation. Romans 8:28 states, "We know that in all things God works for the good of those who love Him, who have been called according to His purpose." I Thessalonians 5:6-18 puts it this way, "Be joyful always; pray continually; give thanks in all circumstances; for this is God's Will for you in Christ Jesus." We may not see any benefits initially, but eventually we will observe His handwork come to fruition.

We shouldn't fret about the troubles of this world. Matthew 6:25 avers, "Do not worry about your life." Matthew 6:34 has it this way, "Do not worry about tomorrow." Remember this comforting quote from Romans 8:31, "If God is for us, who can be against us?"

Satan uses our own biases and prejudices to divide us. We shouldn't find fault with other denominations as long as they are Christian. Do you think the Ruler of the Universe cares what race, creed, nationality, ethnicity, or other man-made contrivance we are? He simply loves all of humanity.

The Devil is the Father of Lies and Deception and encourages chaos, disorder, anarchy, lawlessness, pandemonium, dissonance, and cacophony. The genuine Supreme Being is harmonious, melodious, dulcet, and mellifluous. The Prince of Darkness wants to trip humans up by whispering in our ears that the Lord of Lords is not real, or won't forgive us, or doesn't love us. Don't fall for it; nothing can be further from the truth.

What would happen on Judgment Day if all the answers to life's questions and all secrets were revealed? What if a video showing each person's words, thoughts, and actions during his/her lifetime were played in front of everyone? Then we could see Yahweh's Providence in vivid detail.

Through this prison experience, I have become much closer to the Holy One than I would have been on the outside. Consequently, I consider it a blessing that He allowed me to get locked up. The Triune God has a unique way of turning tragedies into miracles, nightmares into dreams, and trials and tribulations into heavenly favors.

I try to spread the Good News throughout the institution and bring others to Christ. Inmates may call me a "Bible thumper" or a "holy roller," but I just take it in stride and wear these designations as a badge of honor. I try to live a pious life so that I won't be labeled a hypocrite by the non-believer community.

We may never completely understand

Jehovah's true essence or what's behind His reasoning. But, as long as we remember, in humbleness, our true relationship to Him and put Him first in our lives, life will be replete with meaning and fulfillment. Jesus is the only path to joy in this life and salvation in the next. He said in John 14:6, "I am the Way, and the Truth, and the Life. No one comes to the Father except through Me."

Chapter 24:

Quilt

It was once described to me that God's Providence is akin to a gigantic quilt, spreading out infinitely in every direction. That is, each of us has our own square, which represents our life. We know and perceive our little corner of the blanket well, but we have a difficult time deciphering the ones surrounding us. Each block is demarcated by a unique color and design, corresponding to the incredible diversity our Creator has made. We are each individuals with various talents to offer the world. The aggregate of this incredible spectrum makes a colorful mosaic.

The Lord perpetually has the entire coverlet

laid out before Him, watching carefully how all the pieces intermingle together. Because we can't see any other boxes, we have no concept of how any one affects any of the others. We can't envision the Grand Scheme of the universe; that ability rests with the King of Kings alone. We can't conceive the impact that one word or action can have on all the other lives around us.

Things happen all the time to us that makes little or no sense. They don't need to because the Man upstairs has our backs at all times. In a patchwork, the myriad sections appear to tell their own stories, independently from the others. It is only when it is spread out in its totality, and viewed all at once, can a perfectly integrated pattern emerge.

No detail, no matter how miniscule, escapes the Supreme Being's knowledge and attention. He knows us better than we know ourselves, and He knows why things happen the way they do. In Romans 5:3-4 it is written, "We also rejoice in our sufferings because we know that suffering produces perseverance; perseverance, character;

and character, hope."

We need to gravitate away from our natural, earthly self. James 4:10 has it like this: "Humble yourselves before the Lord, and He will lift you up." I Peter 3:4 says, "Your inner self, the unfading beauty of a gentle and quiet spirit...is of great worth in God's sight."

Feeling self-righteous and looking down on other people because of their sins are transgressions that the Pharisees especially had a habit of doing. But Jesus warned in Matthew 7:1-2, "Do not judge, or you too will be judged. For in the same way you judge others, and with the measure that you use, it will be measured to you." So it's in our best interests to leave all the judging to the Ultimate and Final Judge. Acts 5:29 tells us that "We must obey God rather than man!"

1 Corinthians 10:26 instructs, "The earth is the Lord's, and everything in it." All organisms share the planet together, and it is critical that the delicate balance of the ecosystem is maintained. That means ensuring that no more

species become extinct.

I have been an animal lover for as long as I can remember. Throughout my entire childhood, we owned a wonderful dog named Dusty. We did everything together, and he was an integral part of our family. Jehovah gave mankind dominion over the animals. We were meant to eat some for food, but not to kill them frivolously. They are worthy of our love and respect. We should be careful not to destroy their habitats, unless it is absolutely necessary.

The needs of humans, however, should be paramount. For example, using mice (or other lab animals) in a controlled scientific experiment is acceptable if it helps us to live safer and healthier lives. Hunting and fishing are fine, as long as the legal limits are respected, because it prevents overcrowding. Outdoorsmen are some of the biggest advocates for wildlife preservation.

One thing that really upsets me is seeing living things in cages. I guess it's because I've been living in one for 25 years, so I can relate. Zoos that allow their animals to roam freely with a lot of natural space are fine. They also have breeding programs for breeds that are threatened by extinction, which is terrific. I have a problem, though, with those that feature wildlife in small, confined areas. Let's have empathy for our fellow earthly inhabitants.

Our lifetimes are short, only an eye blink compared to eternity. Time has no relevance compared to our sojourn in heaven or to our Master because they are eternal. We need to use whatever time is given to us to further the Deity's kingdom. Ephesians 5:1 calls us to "Be imitators of God." 2 Corinthians 6:16 proclaims, "We are the temple of the living God." While 2 Corinthians 5:20 states, "We are therefore Christ's ambassadors."

Only our Maker gives true and lasting fulfillment. Romans 5:1 avers, "Since we have been justified through faith, we have peace with God." I John 3:20-22 has it this way, "God is greater than our hearts...if our hearts do not condemn us, we have confidence before God and receive anything we ask, because we obey His commands and do what pleases Him." Luke 1:37

praises, “For nothing is impossible with God. “James 4:8 promises, “Come near to God and He will come near to you.”

In 2 Corinthians 5:21 Paul wrote, “God made Him Who had no sin to be sin for us, so that in Him we might become the righteousness of God.” Found in verse 19 of the same chapter, “God was reconciling the world to Himself in Christ.”

Our Heavenly Father created the Holy Quilt and has sovereignty and authority in maintaining it. Only He knows exactly how each life fits into the overall pattern, according to His holy purpose. He alone understands how all of our interactions affect each of the corresponding parties. We must each do our part to make the world a better place than we found it and spread the Gospel to all nations. We know that we can have peace, security, hope, and blessed assurance because we reside in the faithful, capable hands of the Holy Quilter.

Chapter 25:

Little Things

Oftentimes it's the little things that can make the biggest, most meaningful difference. Most people are on a quest to feed their egos by pursuing greed, influence, self-promotion, and self-gratification. This path is in direct opposition to the one that the Holy One wants for us.

In Matthew 7:14 Jesus warns, "But small is the gate and narrow the road that leads to life, and only a few find it."

One of my missions is to make other individuals feel better about themselves and build them up in every respect. By consistently praising and encouraging, you can have a positive effect and impact on other lives.

Perform random acts of kindness, compassion, and consideration without expecting any compensation in return. It will make you feel alive inside, and your heart will be overflowing with warmth, goodness, and gratefulness. You should be thankful to the Holy Spirit for giving you the willingness to do good works. I Thessalonians 5:15 reads this way: "Always try to be kind to each other."

Some examples might include: Give a hug to a loved one or a friendly wave to an acquaintance for no reason. Help a sibling by doing a chore that isn't your responsibility. Change a tire for a motorist stranded on the highway. Babysit for a couple so they can have a night out for themselves. Take a neighbor's dog out for a walk. Run an errand for a harried person who doesn't have the time to do it. Let a car in your lane ahead of you on the freeway. Volunteer at an animal or women's shelter. Say a comforting word to a co-worker having a bad day to uplift his/her spirits. Gather the whole family together for dinner, then have lively conversation and entertaining games. Surprise your spouse with a little gift or a night on the town (dining, movie, and dancing). Give your significant other a massage, special meal, or the pick of a favorite activity.

We should demonstrate civility, empathy, and generosity to our fellow man. The Apostle Paul wrote in Galatians 5:22, "The fruit of the Spirit is love, joy, peace, patience, faithfulness, gentleness, and self-control. Against such things there is no law."

We should all nourish our inner child by staying young at heart. That means enjoying life abundantly with the innocence, wonder, fun, enthusiasm, excitement, gullibility, curiosity, naiveté, energy, trust, and faith that children exude. If you've ever been to Disneyland or Disneyworld as a grown-up, then you know what I'm talking about.

Immaturity as an adult is a detrimental trait but never lose the wonderment of the world as seen by a child. You could be missing out on a lot, and it's beneficial to the soul. Our Savior said in Matthew 18:3, "I tell you the truth, unless you change and become like little children, you will never enter the kingdom of heaven."

In the same vein, it's also important to keep your sense of humor, no matter what curveballs are thrown at you. Everybody is faced with trials, tribulations, and heavy burdens to carry. But at the same time, being able to have laughter in your heart, and having the ability to lighten the moods of others, will remind us not to take the time on this earth, or ourselves, too seriously.

A tenet that I try to live by is "sacrifice now, for rewards in the future." I've lived an unpretentious, spartan life. I've never bought a new car, nor lived in anything bigger than a one-bedroom apartment in adulthood. Saving money and doing without luxuries now, can mean being able to afford a new car, a nice home, or a faraway vacation down the road.

By the same token, we can endure the hardships of this existence knowing the blissful paradise with the Lord that awaits us. How comforting it is to know that!

Have you ever noticed how some are always railing about a certain sin in others, when they themselves are struggling with that same transgression? In other words, whatever demon or weakness that has influence over you, is the same one you find fault in those around you. Why is that? Is it because of the intimate familiarity of that iniquity?

One of the most onerous edicts in the Bible is the one for us to love our adversaries, nemeses, and enemies. In Matthew 5:44 it is written, "Love your enemies and pray for those who persecute you."

My confirmation verse was from Psalm 18:2, "The Lord is my Rock, my Fortress and my Deliverer; my God is my Rock, in Whom I take refuge." This passage has been my compass ever since because it has deep meaning for me, and it is so powerful. The Almighty is our sanctuary, no matter what predicament we are in. As the hymn says, "All other ground is sinking sand." Humans can be fickle, capricious, and unpredictable. We need to cling to the never-changing Holy Edifice during the many tempests that come our way.

He is always available when we need Him. Jehovah promised in Joshua 1:5, "I will never leave you nor forsake you." Like the parable to the prodigal son, He is the Heavenly Father standing in the doorway with welcoming, open arms, hoping we will return home if we have backslidden or lost our way.

The Bible is the inerrant Word of God. I believe that every hallowed word has a literal meaning, unless otherwise indicated. Certainly, there are parables and obvious symbolism (such as in the book of Revelation), but it's spiritually dangerous to question, change the intent, or interject your own beliefs via altering the events or the God-breathed words.

Solomon penned in Proverbs 30:5-6, "Every word of God is flawless; He is a shield to those who take refuge in Him. Do not add to His words, or He will rebuke you and prove you a liar." 2 Corinthians 4:2 cautions, "Nor do we distort the Word of God." The author of Psalm 119:160 praises Yahweh: "All your words are true."

As we approach the end of our journey together, did you notice the common thread found throughout the book? At first blush, it may appear that the topics have been quite disparate and have little in common with each other. When you take a closer look, however, you will notice that there is a mention of the Supreme Being intertwined throughout.

We can honor our Master by being obedient to Him and living a decent, honest, righteous, humble lifetime dedicate to the King of Kings. Our Creator is directly involved in our every-day minutiae. We need to continually keep our focus on Him and make Him our highest priority always.

Despite the busyness filled with myriad distractions, The Holy Trinity should color everything we say, do, and think. When we do His Will, everything else falls into place.

We need to have faith and trust in Him completely. If we stay in the Word, pray fervently and often, and let the Lord of Lords be our reason for living, we shall wear the Crown of Life and then lay it at His feet. Fight the good fight! Onward, Christian soldiers!

Chapter 26:

Forgiveness

Someone once said that success is a journey, not a destination. In other words, it's how you live your life that counts, not what you accomplish. I try to "do the right thing" in every given situation. My philosophy is "make each day the best that I can, and do everything out of love and for the glory of the Master."

Getting older brings wisdom, a compendium of gathered knowledge, and a plethora of life experiences. Because of these acquired skills, the well-seasoned should teach and mentor the younger generation.

William Shakespeare said to be true to yourself, and I've bought into that philosophy.

Those who know me know that I am authentic, genuine, and sincere. Being schmaltzy and sentimental equates to caring deeply about others.

I am profoundly saddened that some of my so-called friends, and a few of my relatives, have chosen not to support me during my imprisonment, when I most need them. It's awfully cold-blooded to cross me out of their lives just because I can no longer be of any use to them. If the roles were reversed, I would show loyalty and help them in any way possible.

Hebrews 13:3 admonishes, "Remember those in prison as if you were their fellow prisoners, and those who are mistreated as if you yourselves were suffering." If any of my loved ones who have lost touch with me want to come back into my life, I would welcome them with open arms.

Amazingly, no one has ever physically hurt me or attempted to extort me while being locked up. I pray for a hedge of protection made up of Holy Angels every night, and the Man Upstairs has always answered my prayer. May He always keep His hand on my shoulder.

It feels like I am the unluckiest guy in the world, yet I'm very, very blessed. I never seem to catch a break, but the Lord has been so good to me. I live in profound misery every day in my present circumstances and with my many physical afflictions. My only hope is found in my Redeemer.

Let me share with you a few anecdotes to illustrate what can happen in the joint. I was out working in industry one day, when a guy nonchalantly picked up a solid 4x4 piece of wood. He snuck up behind another inmate and whacked him on the back of his head six times as hard as he could. The victim's pate was dented in, and blood, mixed with brain fluid, poured from his nostrils. He miraculously survived the vicious attack but has permanent brain damage and limited mental capabilities. Apparently, the fool had called the perpetrator a "cho-mo" (child molester) in front of several others, which precipitated the assault.

I have been experiencing a challenging time

dealing with a myriad of health care maladies. I have been diagnosed with diabetes, hypertension, high cholesterol, Parkinson's Disease, kidney irregularities, and probably Chronic Fatigue Syndrome. The fly in the ointment has been in getting health services to test, diagnose, and treat this mélange of illnesses.

They often disregard you, belittle your symptoms, and prescribe the bare minimum of medications in order to save money. Their generic, obligatory order to solve any ailment: "Write a kite or sign up for sick-call." Several times they have put me in life-threatening predicaments by withholding meds from me without notifying me first, and without providing any explanation!

The soulless DOC has even been known to release prisoners early when they have terminal illnesses. Not because of any humanitarian gesture, but only so they wouldn't have to absorb the cost of open-heart surgery, radiation and chemotherapy, or other expensive procedures.

My discipline record has been immaculate for 25 years, save for one minor violation. Here is what happened. I was waiting to go to work in the library one evening when this 300-pound miserable wretch-of-a-guard barked at me, "Give me that necklace!!" The beaded jewelry around my neck held a precious gold cross medallion given to me by my wife. I calmly explained to the splenetic behemoth that the object in question was one of my five protected "religious items" and was not merely a finished hobby-craft project (which would have to be sent out).

She screamed that she didn't care and contentiously demanded it anyway. To placate her, I tossed it to her underhand, at which point she shockingly ordered me to be confined to my cell. The goon squad picked me up and took me to seg. the next morning even though I did nothing wrong.

The following day I met with the director of Due Process, and he said that, after watching the tape from the camera and reading the report, I should never have been sent to the hole in the first place. He didn't even give me LOP and apologized for the officer's unprovoked verbal attack. She should have been fired on the spot for instigating the whole incident, overreacting, and acting unprofessionally.

The most egregious story is when my dying father came to see me during his final days. He was in an incredible amount of pain, and to this day, I still don't know how he rode 140 miles just to say goodbye to me.

I hadn't seen him all year because he wasn't well enough to travel. His muscles had atrophied, and he was severely emaciated. But his face held a beaming smile of joy and peace. He signed up to see me for three hours, but after only thirty minutes, the jailers announced that the visiting room was closing due to an unspecified security matter (which turned out to be nominal).

The unfeeling turnkeys with calcified hearts were unmoved by my plight and did nothing to help. I was beside myself with grief and anger that my final minutes with my beloved parent was going to be truncated so cruelly. I hugged and kissed Daddy and told him that he had always been my hero. I didn't want to ever let go of him.

The jack-booted thugs transported me a few days later to view my dad's body, but I could have absolutely no contact with any of my family members at the funeral home–not even a comforting word, a wave of acknowledgement, or a hug. During my sixty minutes in front of the casket, under close scrutiny, they would not even take off my handcuffs or my shackles! While enduring the most profound grief of my life, those malevolent, petrous C.O.'s did not show me one iota of compassion.

A message that has been a source of great comfort is "And this too shall pass." Knowing that this intense suffering will someday end gives me the hope needed to endure this nightmare. With heaven promised to me (and all believers) by the Supreme Being, I optimistically say, "In the end, we will win."

The females in my life have given me a tremendous amount of joy, love, and compassion. I've had the honor and privilege of having relationships with 81 attractive women. They included girls during high school, collegiate coeds, workplace colleagues, and social girlfriends. Each one is special to me in her own unique way. Some were introductory dates to get more acquainted, while others blossomed into serious romances (including engagements and/or marriages). You ladies have enhanced my life with caring, tenderness, merriment, affection, and passion. I will never forget any of you, and you will always own a piece of my heart.

True forgiveness was demonstrated to mankind by Jesus Christ, Who, while nailed to the cross, showed Holy Compassion by asking His Father to forgive His executioners. Colossians 3:13 exhorts us to, "Forgive as the Lord forgave you." Matthew 6:14-15 warns, "For if you forgive men when they sin against you, your Heavenly Father will also forgive you. But if you do not forgive men their sins, your Father will not forgive your sins."

I decided many years ago to no longer hold grudges, and to do away with any hatred, animosity, or bitterness in my soul. My metamorphosis has proven quite cathartic, and has freed me from carrying a heavy emotional burden on a daily basis.

I am heartily sorry for every sin I have ever committed, whether it be by commission or omission, and whether it be through my words, thoughts, or actions. I strongly regret and am extremely remorseful for any hurt, denigration, or sorrow that I've caused anyone, at any time, at any place, for any reason. I humbly ask for the Holy Deity's absolution and amnesty from those whom I've offended. By the same token, I pardon anyone who has ever done me wrong or has harmed me in any way.

We can find assurance by reading Psalm 46:10: "Be still, and know that I am God." Many of the great figures in the Bible were arrested and/or incarcerated. Despite their dire circumstances, they overcame evil to fulfill their destiny.

Chapter 8 in the book of Romans is chock-full of words by which to live. Verse 1 proclaims, "Therefore, there is no condemnation for those who are in Christ Jesus." Verses 6-8 has it this way, "The mind of sinful man is death, but the mind controlled by the Spirit is life and peace; the sinful mind is hostile to God. It does not submit to God's laws, nor can it do so. Those controlled by the sinful nature cannot please God." Verse 16 avers, "The Spirit Himself testifies with our spirit that we are God's children."

Verse 18 reassures us, "I consider that our present sufferings are not worth comparing to the glory that will be revealed in us." Verses 29-30 explains, "For those God foreknew He also predestined to be conformed to the likeness of His Son...Those He predestined, He also called; those He called, He also justified; those He justified, He also glorified."

Verse 32 pledges, "He Who did not spare His own Son, but gave Him up for all–how will He not also, along with Him, graciously give us all things?" Verses 37-39 have this beautiful sentiment, "In all these things we are more than conquerors through Him Who loved us. For I am convinced that neither death nor life, neither angels nor demons, neither the present nor the future, nor any powers, neither height nor depth, nor anything else in all creation, will be able to separate us from the love of God that is in Christ Jesus our Lord."

The signs that were prophesied heralding Jesus' return seem to be happening in our present day. That wondrous rapture might very well happen in our lifetimes. 1 Thessalonians 4:16-17 foretells it: "For the Lord Himself will come down from heaven, with a loud command, with the voice of the archangel and the trumpet call of God, and the dead in Christ will rise first. After that, we who are still alive and are left will be caught up together with them in the clouds to meet the Lord in the air." We should be watchful, expectant, and full of exhilarating anticipation for this momentous occasion.

After all the Christians are raptured, a terrible tribulation will come upon the earth for seven years. There will be death, destruction, war, pestilences, and plagues on a scale never seen before.

All of the physical, temporal pleasures of this world pale in comparison to the spiritual satisfaction and fulfillment of having the Lords of Lords as ruler of your life and the promised bliss in the hereafter.

In paradise, we will have new, pure bodies which will never get sick, tired, injured, or worn out. We will commune with and worship all three persons of the Trinity: Father, Son, and Holy Spirit. We will be re-united with our family members and friends, and we will fellowship with all the saints throughout antiquity. Finally, we will rejoice and sing paeans with all those wonderful, powerful cherubim and seraphim who helped us so much during our mortal lives. What a celebration it will be! And it will last for eternity!

The celestial realm will be awesome. 1 Corinthians 2:9 states, "No eye has seen, no ear has heard, no mind has conceived what God has prepared for those who love Him." Jesus will be so radiant that He alone will provide all the light that is needed. He will be the SONshine.

We will each have our own mansion and the streets will be paved with gold. The animals will be tame, gentle, and may even be able to talk. Even our favorite pets will be there to provide us with abundant joy.

There will be no prisons, no jails, no guards, no tears, no disease, no anguish, no evil, no sin, and no death. It will be total peace, harmony, joy, and love.

My personal motto is "I love the King of Kings with all my heart, mind, body, soul, spirit, and every fiber of my being. I love my family, relatives, and friends; I've been favored with the very best ones. I love every person in the world (but that doesn't mean I like everybody) because each one is special to our Maker and is made in His image."

My main priority is to further the Almighty's Kingdom. To accomplish this, I glorify my Creator, spread His Gospel, win souls for Christ, and proselytize to the unbelievers by planting seeds of faith. The Holy Ghost, depending on His supreme Will, may germinate those seeds. This is also my mission in writing this book. I want to live a humble, generous, selfless life devoted to the Holy One, according to His plan.

Live for Jehovah, repent of your sins, invite Yahweh into your heart as your personal Savior, and you will live forever in ecstasy with the Divine One.

I would like to close with the prayer that I say each night, with a few modifications: Heavenly Father, please forgive all my sins. I sincerely repent of each one. Help me lead a good and righteous life, and help me show love toward everyone I meet–even my enemies. Please be with my family, friends, relatives, and myself. Keep us all safe, strong, healthy, and close to You spiritually.

O Triune God, I lift You up and magnify Your holy name, giving You all the praise, glory, laud, honor, adoration, and worship. For only You are worthy. You are the one true God in all the cosmos and You created everything. You are all-knowing, all-powerful, and everywhere, and in You I place all my faith and trust. I freely give You my soul, mind, body, spirit, and everything else I have, to do with me as You will. All other gods are false, dead, man-made, and ersatz.

Cover me with Your priceless blood on Judgment Day, so I may stand before You, holy and unblemished, with all my sins, iniquities, and transgressions forgiven, forgotten, cleansed, and washed away. Thank you, Jesus! Hallelujah! Hosanna in the highest! Please write my name in the Lamb's Book of Life, so I may go to heaven and be with You forever in Your Kingdom, praising Your holy name for eternity.

Fill me with Your Holy Spirit. Let me feel Your goodness, gladness, joy, peace, and holiness that can only come from You. Let me draw closer to You each day, learn more about You each day, and increase in faith in You each day. Your will be done, for Yours is absolute and You see the big picture. Guide me, lead me, mold me, show me what You want me to do, and I will follow You.

Take away all the burdens I'm carrying: the worries, anxieties, fears, negative and evil thoughts, words, and deeds. Take away all the frustrations, bitterness, anger, and hatred inside my heart. Replace them with an overwhelming sense of peace, calmness, contentedness, serenity, tranquility, joy, happiness, and hope. Shower me with wisdom, knowledge, grace, mercy, peace, love, forgiveness, humbleness, and all other blessings.

Surround me with Your legions of Holy Angels to keep me safe from all harm, whether it be physical, mental, emotional, or spiritual. Protect me from Satan, his demons, and anyone who would do harm to me. You are mightier than all that evil put together. I am in awe of Your majesty, power, and strength.

I place myself into Your Mighty Hands. Lift me up and carry me because I am weak and You are strong. I can't make it without You. I submit to You at all times, in all places, in all ways. Please make all the decisions for me in my life, big or small. Help me so I don't get into any kind of trouble, such as going to the hole, getting LOP, or losing my job.

I appreciate, Lord Jesus, all you've done for me. You are the only reason I've been safe all this time. In Your precious Name I pray, and through

Your precious blood, amen.

I am grateful that you took this trek with me. Writing this composition has been a labor of love. It took over fifteen years to complete, including an eight-year hiatus. I wrote this volume entirely on an old, antique typewriter because I had no access to a computer.

The Great Author gave me the words and topics for this discourse and first inspired me to write it in the early 90s. He provided the content, what the cover should look like, who the publisher should be, and what the final product should look like. The Godhead deserves the credit because the entire project stems from Him.

This is the end of our excursion together. I wish I had the opportunity to get to know you, if I don't already. Hopefully, you can now better understand where I'm coming from, and have a better idea what the scene is like for a convict.

May each person who reads this publication receive a special blessing. My prayer is that people will be brought to the Ruler of the Universe through His Holy Spirit. Please give your life to

Him today (if you haven't already) because you don't know when your soul will be asked of you. No one is promised tomorrow, so each breath you take is a gift.

The Doxology: "Praise God from Whom all blessings flow; praise Him, all creatures here below; praise Him above, ye heavenly host; praise Father, Son, and Holy Ghost." Amen.

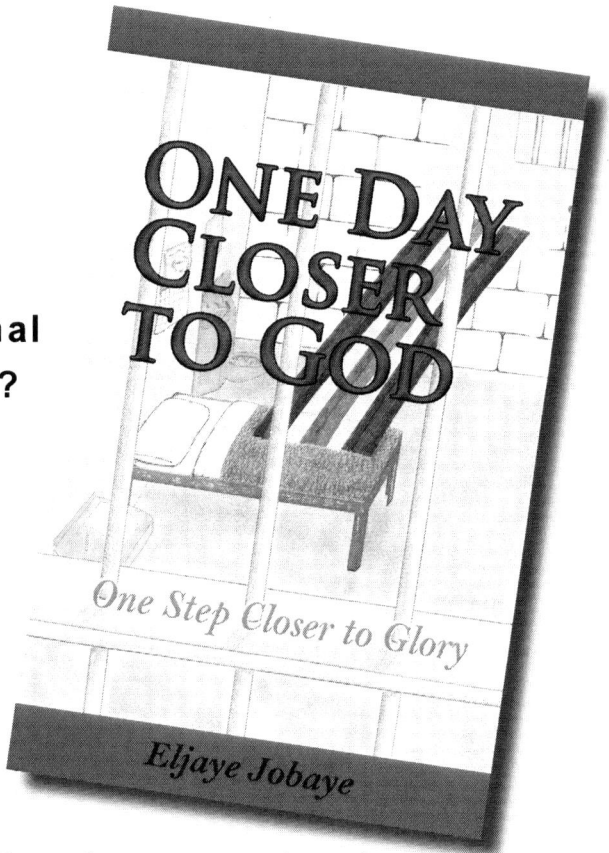